REUTERS

Glossary of International Economic and Financial Terms

Coward-McCann, Inc.
New York

56943

Library of Congress Cataloging in Publication Data

Main entry under title:

Reuters glossary of international
  economic and financial terms.

    1. Commerce — Dictionaries. 2. International
economic relations — Dictionaries. 3. International
finance — Dictionaries. I. Reuters ltd. II. Title:
International glossary of international economic
and financial terms.
HF1001.R48   1982   330'.03   82-14133
ISBN 0-698-11205-9

Printed in the United States of America

FOREWORD

Reuters staff of over 500 journalists produces news services which are distributed in more than 150 countries.

One of Reuters specialities is economic and financial news. Reuters compiled a reference book on economic and financial terms for its own staff, but also received enquiries from its subscribers for a guide to the technical terms used in its specialised business services. Reuters therefore decided to publish a glossary of economic and financial terms for the use of its staff, its subscribers, and the many others who we believed would find the information of value.

I should like to thank those organisations which helped in the compilation of this book.

GLEN RENFREW
Managing Director

August 1982

ACKNOWLEDGMENTS

Senior executives of the following organisations read the manuscripts of this Glossary and sent us suggestions:

London Commodity Exchange Co. Ltd
Grain and Feed Trade Association Ltd
London Metal Exchange
Asian Development Bank
New York Stock Exchange
Chemical Bank
Goldman Sachs & Co.
American Institute of Certified Public Accountants
Securities Industry Association
Commodity Exchange Inc.
Chicago Board of Trade

Many of the suggestions have been incorporated in the final compilation.

Responsibility for the contents of the Glossary rests entirely with Reuters.

AA

'Always afloat', a marine chartering term. The charterer accepts the ship will always be afloat during the charter period whether it is in port or at sea, in order to avoid damage to the hull.

AAA

Top rating for bonds (primarily US corporate and municipal) of the highest quality awarded by Standard and Poor's or by Moody's, the two principal US rating companies.

A 1

Originally a shipping term, but now given a wider meaning of 'in perfect condition' or 'first class'.

ABANDONMENT

Used when a ship is abandoned as dangerous or unseaworthy; normally implies the vessel is a total loss.

ABOVE THE LINE

That part of a government budget concerned with revenue, mainly taxes and expenditure. A treasury or finance ministry normally budgets for a surplus above the line for demand management purposes. For corporations it means all income and expense items before tax. See BELOW THE LINE.

ACCELERATED DEPRECIATION

Accrual of depreciation under a method that results in reporting a decreasing amount of depreciation expense each year over the life of the asset.

ACCEPTANCE CREDIT

An exporter or importer may obtain funds from a bank arranging for it to accept bills of exchange drawn on it by him. The bills can then be sold, as the bank's acceptance means the buyer of the bills can look to the bank for payment.

ACCEPTANCE HOUSE

Financial institution lending money on the security of bills

Ac

of exchange. It may lend money on a bill, or add its name to a bill drawn on another party, especially in foreign trade. Acceptance houses often lend money to an exporter to cover the gap between the production of goods and the receipt of proceeds from their sale. The loan is made through a bill of exchange and is sometimes called an acceptance credit.

ACCEPTING HOUSES COMMITTEE
The 17 leading London merchant banks. Bills of exchange drawn on them are discountable at fine rates. The Committee also ensures policy co-ordination between its members, the Treasury and the Bank of England. See FINE RATES.

ACCEPTOR
Drawee who signs a bill of exchange and thereby undertakes to pay the bill at its maturity.

ACCESSION COMPENSATORY AMOUNTS (ACA)
Monetary amounts which take account of differences between full EC Common Agricultural Policy (CAP) prices and prices fixed for new member states during their transition. ACAs apply to trade and to support prices until prices in the new member states are aligned with full CAP prices.

ACCESSION RATE
Additional employees hired as a percentage of total employment. Also called hiring rate.

ACCOMMODATION PAPER
Bill of exchange signed by one person to oblige another. The person signing becomes guarantor, but receives no consideration. If the acceptor fails to pay, the guarantor becomes liable. Such bills are considered first class in Britain as there is no physical collateral.

ACCOMMODATION PLATFORM
Platform or semi-submersible rig built or adapted to act as quarters for offshore personnel. Oil term.

ACCOUNT

(a) In the UK, period, usually of two successive weeks during which stock exchange deals are done for settlement on account day. There are 24 account periods in a year.

(b) In the US, a broker's record of a customer's transactions.

ACCOUNT DAY

Also called SETTLEMENT DAY in the UK. The day on which all bargains for the account are settled. The account day is usually a Tuesday.

ACCRETION

Addition of principal or interest to a fund over a period as the result of an accumulation plan. In portfolio accounting, discount bonds are accreted to par, while premium bonds are amortised to par.

ACCRUED INTEREST

Interest due from issue or from the most recent coupon date to the present on an interest bearing security. If the security is sold, the price is adjusted to take into account accrued interest.

ACCUMULATED DEPRECIATION

Total depreciation expense accrued from the date of purchase to the present.

ACH

Automated Clearing House. A US computer based clearing and settlement operation often operated by a Federal Reserve bank, established for the exchange of electronic (i.e. paperless) transactions among participating depository institutions.

ACID TEST RATIO

Simple ratio of a company's liquid assets to current liabilities. Such assets include cash, marketable securities and accounts receivable.

Ac

ACP STATES
African, Caribbean and Pacific states which under the terms of the 1975 Lomé Agreement receive preferential terms in trade with the EC.

ACQUISITION
Takeover of one company by another.

ACREAGE ALLOTMENT
US government limitation on the planted acreage of some crops.

ACROSS THE BOARD TARIFF NEGOTIATIONS
Negotiations involving uniform percentage reductions or increases in duties on major categories of items. The opposite is item by item tariff negotiation.

ACSA
American Cotton Shippers Association.

ACT OF GOD
Used in contracts for a direct, irresistible, unpreventable act of nature.

ACTUAL TOTAL LOSS
Used in insurance, especially marine insurance, implying complete destruction. It can be presumed if a ship is missing.

ACTUALS
Also called PHYSICALS. Refers to the physical commodities. Physicals which are available for delivery are traded for cash on a spot or forward basis as opposed to futures contracts, which are traded on MARGIN.

AD VALOREM
Tax or duty levied as a fixed percentage of an item's value as opposed to a fixed unitary levy e.g. stamp duties.

Ad

ADB
African Development Bank, based in Abidjan and founded in 1964.

ADB
Asian Development Bank, based in Manila and founded in 1966.

ADDRESS COMMISSION
Commission paid to the charterer's agent for arranging the loading of the vessel. Shipping term.

ADJUSTABLE PEG
Exchange rate regime in which a currency is 'pegged' or 'fixed' in relation to another currency, frequently the US dollar, with the rate being adjusted from time to time.

ADJUSTED CIF PRICE
Used by the EC in calculating its variable import levy. See CIF.

ADJUSTMENT
Change in the official currency rate or in internal economic policies to correct a payments imbalance.

ADJUSTMENT PROCESS
International system and operation of payments adjustment policies e.g. exchange rate alignment, changes in government expenditure, exchange controls.

ADJUSTMENT TRIGGER
Objective criterion impelling exchange rate or economic policy adjustment.

ADR
See AMERICAN DEPOSITARY RECEIPTS.

ADVANCE FREIGHT
Freight paid in advance. It enables the shipper to endorse the

bill of lading with a freight release, and the importer to take immediate delivery.

ADVANCE REFUNDING
Extension of public debt before maturity.

ADVERSE BALANCE
Balance of payments deficit.

ADVISORY FUNDS
Funds placed with a bank or other financial institution to invest at its own discretion on the client's behalf.

AFESD
Arab Fund for Economic and Social Development, based in Kuwait and established in 1968.

AFFREIGHTMENT
Contract of Affreightment (COA). The provision of a certain tonnage capacity to transport bulk cargo during a specific period between two ports or areas at agreed rates.

AFLOAT
Goods on the high seas en route to their destination. Does not apply to arrivals ready for unloading.

AFTER HOURS TRADING
Trading based on rules and terms of an equity, futures or terminal market after the official close of the market.

AFTER SIGHT
Bill of exchange drawn after sight is payable when it has been accepted and the acceptor has written an acceptance date on the bill.

AFTER TAX REAL RATE RETURN
Net yield obtained from nominal rate of return after tax minus the inflation rate.

AFTERDATE
A bill of exchange payable at a certain time after the date of the bill.

AG
Arabian Gulf. Shipping term.

AGAINST ACTUALS
See EXCHANGE FOR PHYSICAL.

AGAINST ALL RISKS (AAR)
Insured against all generally accepted risks in marine insurance.

AGENCY BANK
Form of organisation frequently used by foreign banks to enter the US market. An agency bank is unable to accept deposits or extend loans in its own name. It acts as agent for the parent bank.

AGENCY FEE
Charge by a ship's agent or shipowner for services while the ship is in port.

AGENT BANK
Bank appointed by members of an international lending syndicate to protect the lenders' interests during the life of a loan. Similar to the trustee of a bond issue.

AGGREGATE DEMAND
Total demand for goods and services in the economy. It comprises household demand for consumer goods and services; demand from firms and government for investment goods; demand by local and central government for goods and services; demands of consumers and firms in other countries for goods and services, i.e. exports.

Ag

AGGREGATE RISK

Total exposure of a bank to any single customer for both spot and forward contracts.

AGGREGATE SUPPLY

Total supply of goods and services in the economy available to meet aggregate demand. This is made up of domestically produced goods and imports.

AGIO

Difference in value between currencies. Also used as a term to describe the percentage charged on changing paper money into cash, or a weak currency into a strong currency.

AGREEMENT AMONGST UNDERWRITERS

Legal document binding an underwriting group into a syndicate. In the US it is normally between the borrower (issuer) and all the underwriters. In the UK and Eurobond markets it may be limited to an agreement between managing underwriters, who then make sub-underwriting agreements with other underwriters.

A/H

Ports of Antwerp and Hamburg. Shipping term.

AIBD

Association of International Bond Dealers based in Zurich.

AKA

Ausfuhrkredit GmbH. Export credit company formed by a consortium of all West German commercial banks to provide medium and long term export finance.

ALADI

Asociación Latino-Americana de Intergración (Latin American Integration Association). Due to replace the Latin American Free Trade Area (LAFTA) early in 1983 with a less ambitious but more flexible association. Its members will be split into three categories: the most developed (Argentina, Brazil and Mexico), the intermediate (Chile, Colombia, Peru,

Uruguay and Venezuela) and less developed (Bolivia, Ecuador, and Paraguay). Its aims are to establish a system of bilateral preference agreements taking into account the different development stages of member countries. See LAFTA.

ALL IN COST
Total costs, both explicit and others.

ALL OR NONE
Market or limited price order requiring that no part of an order be executed unless all of it can be executed at the specified price.

ALLONGE
Slip attached to a bill of exchange for the purpose of receiving endorsements.

ALLOTMENT
Allocation of securities from a new issue. If the issue proves popular, the allotment may be made as a percentage of the amount of shares applied for. In the Eurobond and US securities markets, it refers to the allocation of securities to members of the syndicate involved in the issue.

ALLOTMENT LETTER
Informs the addressee of the number of shares he has been allotted. The letter is of value and may act as a temporary or permanent certificate.

ALLOWANCES
Discounts or premiums to par allowed for commodity grades or delivery locations which differ from the basis grade or location specified in a futures contract. Also called differentials.

ALONGSIDE
Goods delivered alongside a ship for delivery to the dock or lighter from which they can be loaded aboard.

A1

ALTERNATIVE ORDER
Order to do either of two alternatives, e.g. either sell or buy a particular stock at a limit price.

AMERICAN DEPOSITARY RECEIPTS (ADR)
Issued by US banks to facilitate trading in foreign stocks or shares.

AMERICAN SELLING PRICE (ASP)
Procedure allowing the US to impose import tariffs of over 100% on imported chemicals without appearing to do so by basing the tariff on the value of the US domestic product, not the value of the import.

AMEX
American Stock Exchange.

AMORTISATION
Gradual redemption of a debt through a periodic repayment of principal and interest. Often includes use of a sinking fund.

AMSTEL CLUB
Grouping of finance houses from 15 European countries which make reciprocal arrangements to finance trade, especially for the smaller exporter. The official title is Amstel Finance International AG.

ANCHORAGE
Dues to be paid for anchoring in certain harbours and ports.

ANHYDROUS AMMONIA
'Dry' ammonia, i.e. ammonia containing no dissolved water. It is one of the most important petroleum-derived raw materials used in the chemical industry.

API GRAVITY
Universally accepted scale adopted by the American Petroleum Institute for expressing the specific gravity of oils:

$$\text{API gravity} = \frac{141.5}{\text{specific gravity at } 60^\circ \text{ F}} - 131.5$$

API gravity serves as a rough measure of quality, i.e. the higher the API gravity number, the richer the yield in premium refined products. Saudi Arabian Light has an API gravity of 34, whilst Algerian Saharan has an API gravity of 44.

APPLICATION FORM
Special form used when applying for securities offered for sale.

APPLIED PROCEEDS SWAP
Proceeds from the sale of a block of bonds in the US which are then used in buying another block of bonds.

APPRAISAL DRILLING
Drilling carried out to establish the physical extent, reserves and likely production rate of an oil or gas field.

APPRECIATION
Increase in market value of a capital asset, financial paper or a currency's exchange rate.

APPROVED DELIVERY FACILITY
Any bank, stockyard, mill, store, warehouse, plant, elevator or other depositary recognised by an exchange as approved for the delivery of commodities tendered against a future contract.

APPROVED SECURITIES
Securities or obligations of states etc. which are approved for holding by banks and financial institutions as part of their reserves or similar requirements.

APS
Arrival Pilot Station. Shipping term.

ARA
Ports of Antwerp/Rotterdam/Amsterdam. Shipping term.

ARAB BANK FOR ECONOMIC DEVELOPMENT IN AFRICA (ABEDA)
Established in 1973 and based in Khartoum.

Ar

ARAB MONETARY FUND

Based in Abu Dhabi and formed in 1977 by the Council for Arab Economic Unity. Members are Saudi Arabia, Algeria, Bahrain, Iraq, Jordan, Kuwait, Lebanon, Libya, Mauritania, Morocco, Oman, Qatar, Somalia, Sudan, Syria, United Arab Emirates, Tunisia, Yemen Arab Republic, People's Democratic Republic of Yemen and the Palestine Liberation Organisation. Egypt's membership was suspended in April 1979.

ARBITRAGE

Simultaneous purchase of foreign exchange, securities or commodities in one market and sale in another (at a higher price) or the simultaneous matching of trades in one commodity on two markets, or a profitable spot or forward exchange transaction to exploit yield differentials in different centres.

ARBITRATION

Settlement of a difference usually arising from a contract by referring the dispute to one or more independent persons rather than instituting formal legal proceedings. Arbitration must be agreed and cannot be imposed. It tends to be simpler, quicker, and cheaper than legal proceedings.

ARCRU

Unit of account based on the movement of eight Arab currencies against the US dollar. Introduced in 1974, it originally comprised twelve currencies and was worth one US dollar. Subsequently, the two weakest and two strongest currencies were eliminated from the basket with the unit's value then calculated from an average valuation of the remainder. The eight currencies are those of Kuwait, Bahrain, Saudi Arabia, Qatar, United Arab Emirates, Oman, Iraq, Lebanon, Syria, Egypt, Libya and Algeria.

AROUND

Foreign exchange market term to quote forward premiums or discounts with the par point understood, e.g. ten-ten around means ten points on either side of par, i.e. the current spot rate.

ARTICLE EIGHT CURRENCY
A 'senior currency' according to the IMF definition. It should be convertible and free from controls.

ASA
American Soybean Association representing US soybean producers.

ASEAN
Association of South East Asia Nations formed in 1967 with its headquarters in Jakarta. Members are Malaysia, Indonesia, Singapore, Philippines, Thailand.

AS IF AND WHEN
Provided a transaction takes place at the agreed time. Finance and shipping term.

ASIAN CLEARING UNION
Joint arrangement for settling international payments imbalances between Bangladesh, Burma, India, Iran, Nepal, Pakistan and Sri Lanka. The Asian Monetary Unit is used as the unit of account.

ASIAN CURRENCY UNIT (ACU)
Separate accounting unit used in Singapore by selected banks licensed to deal in non-resident deposits.

ASIAN DOLLARS
US dollar bank deposits normally held in Asia and traded outside the US, similar to Eurodollars. The market is based in Singapore.

ASIAN DOLLAR BONDS
Similar to Eurobonds, but based in Singapore. The market emerged following the successful development of the Asian dollar market.

ASIAN MONETARY UNIT
Accounting unit for the Asian Clearing Union with a value equal to the Special Drawing Rights (SDR) issued by the International Monetary Fund.

As

ASKED
Price at which a security, commodity etc. is offered for sale or the rate at which a loan is offered. Opposite is the bid price.

ASPA
American Soybean Processors Association. Represents US soybean crushers.

AS PER ADVICE
Indicates the drawee of a bill of exchange has been notified that the bill has been drawn on him.

ASSAY
To assess qualitatively and quantitatively the purity of metals. The former is mainly used to assess the fineness of precious metals, and the latter by mining companies in assessing the potential of ore bodies.

ASSETS
What a company owns or is owed. Cash, investments, monies due, material and stock are equivalent to current assets. Plant, machinery and properties are fixed assets. A third category, intangible assets, is represented by patents and goodwill.

ASSOCIATED GAS
Natural gas found in association with oil.

ASSOCIATED LIQUIDS
Liquid hydrocarbons found in association with natural gas.

ASSOCIATION CAMBISTE INTERNATIONALE
The International Association of Foreign Exchange dealers based in Paris.

ASTM
American Society for Testing Materials. Responsible for issuing many of the standard methods used in the oil industry.

14

AT AND FROM
Marine insurance covering a ship at sea and in port.

AT BEST
Instruction with a buying or selling order indicating it should be carried out immediately at the best possible price. Also known as 'at the market'.

AT CALL
Money or funds at call, i.e. immediately available.

ATDONSHINC
'Any time day or night Sundays and holidays inclusive'. Shipping term.

AT OR BETTER
Instruction to trade at a specific level or better.

AT PAR
Nominal or face value of a share or security. In the case of a US debt security usually refers to value at maturity.

AT SIGHT
Describes a bill of exchange payable on presentation rather than on a specific date.

AT THE CLOSE
Market order to be executed as near to the close as possible.

AT THE MARKET
See AT BEST.

AT THE OPENING
Market order to be executed at the opening or not at all.

AUTHENTICITY
In the gold markets, the actual gold content of any lot in hand and authenticated by a reliable seller.

Au

AUTHORISED CAPITAL/STOCK
Maximum amount of all classes of stocks and shares which a company is authorised to issue by its shareholders, but different from issued capital.

AUTHORISED DEALER
Bank, financial institution authorised by government agency or central bank to deal in foreign exchange. It can also cover authorisation to deal in securities or commodities for traders in these sectors.

AUTHORITY TO PURCHASE/NEGOTIATE
Used especially in trade with the Far East. A bill is drawn on the buyer and presented with shipping documents to the London bank acting for the purchaser's bank. If the documents are in order, the London bank buys the bill from the exporter.

AVAL
Payment of a bill of exchange or a promissory note which is guaranteed by the signature of a third person on the bill. European term.

AVERAGE LIFE
Maturity of a borrowing after taking into account repayments or purchases by the borrower's sinking fund.

AVERAGING
Extra purchases or sales of shares, stocks or commodities at different prices thus adjusting the average price; it can also mean making regular purchases through investing a fixed amount in a security etc. with the amount of stock received depending on the price level (known as dollar cost averaging in the US).

AVIATION TURBINE KEROSENE (ATK)
Medium-light fuel burned in jet and turbo-prop aircraft engines.

AWAY
US term for a trade, quote or market that does not approximate to current market levels.

Ba

B

BACK
Abbreviation for BACKWARDATION.

BACK TO BACK CREDIT
Credit opened by a finance house or bank on the strength of another credit and used in foreign trade. The foreign importer provides the finance house with the relevant documents, on the strength of which a credit is opened in favour of the exporter. These can then be used to back another credit for the exporter, i.e. the first credit backs the second.

BACK TO BACK LOAN
Arrangement whereby a loan in the currency of one country is set against a loan in another country's currency. It can be used to avoid or overcome exchange risks and controls, although interest rate differentials may cause problems. See SWAP.

BACKED NOTE
Note authorising a ship's master to take on water-borne goods and evidence that freight charges are covered.

BACKING AND FILLING
Speculative market with numerous small rises and falls, but without any overall major change in price levels.

BACKING SUPPORT
Gold or silver securities used to support a state's note issue.

BACKWARDATION
(a) On commodity markets a situation where the cash or near delivery price is at a premium to the price for forward delivery i.e. opposite to contango. It is used in the same way on foreign exchange markets.
(b) On the London Stock Exchange, the percentage cost paid by a seller of stock to delay delivery.

BAIL BOND
Bond given to a court to secure the release of an arrested vessel.

Ba

BALANCE CERTIFICATE
Certificate issued to a shareholder when he has sold only part of the shares represented by a share certificate.

BALANCE FOR OFFICIAL FINANCING
Used in UK balance of payments statistics, and comprises current account balance, total investment and other capital flows plus a balancing item covering errors and omissions. It is equal to the changes in the reserves together with total official borrowing or lending.

BALANCE OF PAYMENTS
Systematic record of one country's net transactions with the rest of the world over a given period. It includes trade, services, capital movements and unilateral transfers.

BALANCE OF TRADE
Monetary record of a country's net imports and exports of physical merchandise.

BALANCE SHEET
Summary of assets and liabilities at a given date. It is not an exact statement of financial position as the figures are a mix of fact and estimate reflecting the position as fairly and accurately as possible.

BALANCE SHEET RATIOS
Extracted from the balance sheet, these provide information about a company's performance. Important ratios include the liquidity ratio, gross profit as a percentage of turnover, net profit as a percentage of gross profit, the level of credit given compared to turnover, and the rate of stock turnover.

BALANCED BUDGET
Budgetary situation where expenditure matches revenue. Also called a neutral budget.

BALE CAPACITY
Cubic capacity of a space when the breadth is taken from

inside the cargo battens, the depth from the wood ceiling to the underside of the deck beams and the length from inside the bulk head stiffeners or sparring where fitted. Shipping term.

BALE CARGO
Goods wrapped in burlap or similar material for shipment overseas.

BALLAST BONUS (BB)
Lump sum figure paid to cover a voyage in ballast i.e. without cargo.

BALLOON
Loan where the last repayment is much larger than the other repayments, or where all the loan is repaid at maturity.

BALTIC EXCHANGE
London exchange which is one of the largest freight markets in the world, engaged in matching cargoes to ships and vice versa and covering both seaborne and air freight. It is also a centre of grains and oilseed trading.

BAND
Maximum permitted range within which a currency is allowed to move against a reference currency. See EMS.

BANK BILL
Bill of exchange issued or accepted by a bank. It is thus more acceptable than a normal trade bill as the risk is less, while the discount is also smaller.

BANK DEPOSIT
Money held by a bank on behalf of a private, corporate, banking or government customer. It appears in the bank's accounts as a liability.

BANK FOR INTERNATIONAL SETTLEMENTS (BIS)
Profit making clearing agency based in Basle for central bank

shareholder members in foreign exchange and Eurocurrency markets. The US Federal Reserve Board (FRB) is not a member for technical reasons, and the US shareholding is through Citibank. The BIS acts as principal forum for routine meetings of central bank governors (always attended by an FRB member). Its financial accounts are denominated in Swiss gold francs. Dividends are paid annually in dollars at the day's Zurich Swiss franc spot rate.

BANK HOLDING COMPANY

US term for a company which owns or controls one or more banks. The Federal Reserve Board has responsibility for regulating and supervising such companies.

BANK RATE

Official discount rate set by a central bank. See DISCOUNT RATE. Sometimes refers to the interest rate charged by a commercial bank on typical loans.

BANK RELEASE

Issued by a bank after being paid on a bill of exchange and enables the purchaser of the goods to take delivery.

BANK RETURN

Weekly or monthly statement issued by a central bank showing its financial position in summary form.

BANKERS ACCEPTANCE

Negotiable time draft drawn on and accepted by a bank which adds its credit to that of an importer of merchandise. It typically arises from letters of credit in foreign trade. The posted rate is an indicated rate that many foreign banks use to finance letters of credit. It is not a real indication of the rates in the dealer market and is used as a rate for small transactions. The bank offered rate is the rate at which the bank is willing to transact business in the market.

BANKERS DRAFT

Draft payable on demand and drawn by or on behalf of the

bank itself. It is regarded as cash and cannot be returned unpaid. Often used in international trade.

BANKRUPTCY

A company becomes formally bankrupt following a court ruling that it is unable to meet its debts. The ruling may be sought either by the company concerned (voluntary liquidation) or by its creditors. In England an official receiver is appointed by the court to manage and eventually realize the debtors' assets on behalf of the creditors. Different rules and procedures are followed in other countries.

BANQUE D'AFFAIRES

French investment bank, similar to a British merchant bank. It has much greater scope than a US investment bank. See MERCHANT BANK.

BAR

Dealing term for one million sterling on the interbank market.

BARDEPOT

West German regulation which requires a percentage of foreign borrowings by German residents to be deposited in cash in a non-interest bearing account with the Bundesbank.

BAREBOAT CHARTER

Ship charter arranged for a specific period under which the charterer in effect takes control of the vessel, paying all operating and voyage costs.

BARGAIN

Transaction on UK stock exchanges.

BARRATRY

Illegal or fraudulent act commited by the master or crew of ship to the prejudice of the owner or charterer.

BARRELS

Volume measurement of liquid in the petroleum industry. It equals about 0.136 tonnes depending upon specific gravity ranging from 7.1 to 7.8 barrels per tonne. A barrel contains 36 Imperial gallons, 42 US gallons, or 159 litres.

Ba

BARRELS PER DAY (BPD)
Represents the total volume of oil produced from a field, carried through a pipeline, or processed, divided by number of days in the period. One barrel a day is equivalent to around 50 tonnes per annum, depending on specific gravity.

BARTER
Exchange of goods or services for other goods or services. No money is exchanged.

BASE CURRENCY
Currency against which exchange rates are normally quoted in a given centre or country, e.g. the US dollar or sterling.

BASE PRICE
Described under the EC's Common Agricultural Policy as a national support price used to determine the level at which producers or EC governments may support the market.

BASE RATE
Annual interest rate on which graduated lending charges are calculated by British banks.

BASE YEAR
Year chosen as the base for an economic index.

BASIC BALANCE
Balance of payments on current and long term capital account.

BASIC PETROCHEMICAL
Basic raw material manufactured from crude oil by steam cracking or reforming.

BASIC POINT PRICE
System under which delivered prices in a specific industry represent the cost at a number of production centres plus a standard freight charge for the same distance. Prices are thus standard whatever the base used.

BASIS
Differential between the futures price of a commodity and its cash or spot price.

BASIS GRADE

Grade of a commodity used as the standard of the contract.

BASIS POINT

Unit of measure (usually one hundredth of a percentage point) used to express movements in interest rates, foreign exchange rates, or bond yields.

BATTEN FITTED

Pieces of wood fixed above a cargo to keep it in place. Shipping term.

BC

British Columbia. Bulk carrier. Shipping terms.

BEAM

Width of ship.

BEAR

Investor who sells short in the expectation of a decline in a currency, the price of a commodity, stock or bond with the hope of buying it back at a lower price. If he sells something he does not have, he is called an uncovered bear in the UK, shortseller in the US.

BEAR COVERING

Situation where bears who have previously sold a currency, commodity or stock, are now buying them again, i.e. covering themselves. Short covering in the US.

BEAR MARKET

Market in which prices are generally declining and the underlying sentiment reinforces that decline.

BEAR RAID

Heavy shortselling by one or more big traders hoping to depress prices so they can profitably repurchase at lower rates.

BEAR SQUEEZE

Official action by central banks in currency markets to put pressure on 'uncovered bears'. The bank acts to maintain the level of the currency which the bears have sold. Instead of

Be

being able to buy it back at a lower rate, the bears faced with a a need for the currency have to buy back at a higher price than they sold, thus making a loss. Can also occur in other markets, though without official action, e.g. commodity markets.

BEARER
Person possessing a bill or note payable to bearer, i.e. owner-ship is presumed to be with the person bearing or holding the bill or note.

BEARER BOND
Bond in which ownership is transferable to the bearer, rather than registered on the books of the issuer in the name of a particular person. Bearer securities normally have a coupon attached to them which is detached as interest payments become due, and is presented as evidence of the bearer's right to payment.

BEARER DEPOSITARY RECEIPTS
Depositary Receipt in bearer form.

BEARER SECURITY
Security which promises to pay the holder of the security on demand.

BED
Layer of sediments or sedimentary rock of considerable thick-ness and uniform composition and texture.

BELOW THE LINE
That part of a budget concerning receipts relating to the redemption of debt and expenditure to be financed by borrowing.

BENCHMARK
Actual measurement of economic data in a specific time period, used as a basis for comparison.

BENDS
Short for 'both ends'. Shipping term normally used when the

load and discharge of a vessel is the same, or when a description of the load and discharge is the same, such as 'Shex' and 'Shinc'. (See SHEX and SHINC).

BENZENE

Key petroleum-derived raw material used in the chemical industry.

BERNE UNION

Established in 1934 in Berne to study export credit insurance techniques. The full title is the International Union of Credit and Investment Insurers.

BERTH BILL OF LADING

Bill of lading issued by the master of a vessel belonging to a regular shipping line.

BERTH TERMS

Terms under which shipowner pays loading and discharge costs. Also described as gross terms.

BEST EFFORT

US term for a new securities issue which is not underwritten or purchased as a whole but sold on the basis of what can be sold. It can also mean an order to sell currency or securities at the best available price over a given period.

B/H

The ports of Bordeaux/Hamburg. Shipping term.

BHF

Bulk harmless fertilisers. Shipping term.

BID

Undertaking to purchase at a specific price e.g. the rate at which a dealer will buy or borrow a currency; the rate paid for a deposit or security; the price offered by a purchaser in the Eurobond secondary market.

Bi

BID AND ASKED
Highest price a dealer has said he is prepared to pay for a security or commodity at a specific time. The asked price is the lowest that anyone will accept at the same time.

BID MARKET
Market where bids predominate over offers at the ruling market price.

BIG BOARD
New York Stock Exchange price display.

BILATERAL CLEARING
Often used in international trade between developing countries and East Bloc states. Trade and other payments are balanced and settled once yearly by the central banks involved. Settlements often take place in convertible currencies.

BILL BROKER
Firm or individual who buys and sells bills of exchange. The term is interchangeable with a discount house (UK).

BILL OF EXCHANGE
Key negotiable instrument of exchange in international trade. It is an unconditional order in writing addressed by one person to another, signed by the person giving it, requiring the person to whom it is addressed to pay on demand, or at a fixed or determinable future time, a certain sum in money to, or to the order of, a specified person or to the bearer.

BILL OF LADING
Used in foreign trade, to describe fully the details of the goods being sent. A marine bill of lading can give the holder the right of possession to goods and acts as receipt for the goods. In the US and UK it is a negotiable instrument and a document of

title. The shipowner is compelled to release goods to the first presenter of a bill of lading, in the absence of prima facie evidence of fraud.

BILL OF SIGHT

Document for inspection by customs, completed by an importer when unable to provide all details of his cargo.

BIS

See BANK FOR INTERNATIONAL SETTLEMENTS.

BLEEDING

Drawing off at a slow pace a small portion of liquid from a container or vessel.

BLOCK POSITIONER

US term for a securities firm which acquires 'blocks' of securities to facilitate the trading of institutional client demand.

BLOCK TRADING

Transacting large stock lots, usually in excess of 10,000 shares among institutional purchasers or sellers.

BLOCKED ACCOUNTS

Bank accounts where payments cannot be freely made e.g. accounts frozen for political reasons.

BLOCKED CURRENCY

Currency whose use is controlled by the government of issue. Such currency can only be used for purchases within the country.

BLOWOUT

When gas, oil or salt water, usually by accident, escapes from a well due to release of pressure in the reservoir rock not controlled by the containment systems, or to failure of the containment systems during production.

BLUE CHIP

Common stock of companies with proven management skills and expertise. Usually involves major companies with sound earnings and dividend records and above average share performance. Extremely well known and regarded corporations.

BLUE SKY LAWS

US state (not federal) laws enacted to protect the public against securities frauds.

BOARD ORDER

Order to buy (or sell) when a particular price is reached.

BOILING RANGE

Distillation range.

BOND

Usually a fixed interest security under which the issuer contracts to pay the lender a fixed principal amount at a stated date in the future, and a series of interest payments, either semi-annually or annually. Interest payments may vary through the life of a bond. The issuer may be a government, municipal or corporate entity. Bonds maturing in less than five years are described as short term, between six and fifteen years as medium term and more than fifteen as long term. In the US a bond is normally for more than ten years. See also DEBENTURE.

BOND ANTICIPATORY NOTES (BANs)

Notes issued in the US by states and municipalities to provide interim finance for projects to be funded by bond issues.

BOND INDENTURE

Legal document in the US setting out the duties of the issuer and the rights of the holder.

BOND MARKET
Primary or secondary market for government municipal or corporate debt securities. See PRIMARY AND SECONDARY MARKETS.

BOND (PERFORMANCE)
Form of guarantee that if a contract is not carried out as required, an indemnity will be payable, usually by a bank.

BOND YIELD
Rate of annual income return on a bond expressed as a percentage of its price. There are three types of yield— nominal, current, and yield to maturity.

BONUS ISSUE
Issue by a company of shares to existing shareholders and for which cash payment is not required. Normally allocated to shareholders in proportion to their current share-holdings.

BOOK
Term used by dealers for their total exposure to markets, e.g. the total of assets or liabilities in the foreign exchange market.

BOOK ENTRY SECURITIES
Used in the US to refer to securities which are issued and recorded in a computer. All US Treasury Bills are held in this manner.

BOOK VALUE
Value of a corporation or of a corporate asset according to accounting records. Also known as net asset value. It is determined by dividing the number of issued shares into a company's net assets.

BOOKED
Expression for the book-keeping entries connected with a given transaction being entered in a country other than where the transaction takes place. Normally done to lessen tax liability.

Bo

BOOM
Rapid and sustained rise in prices and general business activity.

BORDER TAX ADJUSTMENT
Under GATT rules, border tax adjustments are permitted on internationally traded goods. Exports may be relieved of indirect taxes and imports taxed an amount equivalent to indirect taxes on similar domestic goods. No adjustment is allowed for direct taxes.

BORROWING REQUIREMENT
Net amount of money needed by a government to finance budget deficits and maturing debt.

BOTTOM
Shipping term for a vessel.

BOTTOMRY BOND
If a ship's master requires funds urgently to complete a voyage, he can borrow on the security of the ship and cargo via a bottomry bond. Communication with the owner must be impossible, and no other way of raising money such as using the shipowner's credit must be available.

BOTTOMS
Residue of the heavy portion of the feed in a distillation operation. Storage tank 'bottoms' refers to the accumulation of sediment, mud and water.

BOURSE
French term for stock exchange, grain exchange or exchange dealing in other commodities. Also used to cover traders' meetings.

BOURSE DE COMMERCE
Familiar term for the Paris commodity exchange.

BOURSE DE COMMERCE EUROPEENNE
European Commodities Exchanges Association.

30

BRACKET
Term used in the US and Euromarkets to group the different categories of managers, and underwriters of syndicated loans. The lead manager, co-managers, top underwriter, major underwriters etc. are listed alphabetically within their respective brackets.

BREAK
Rapid and sharp price decline.

BRETTON WOODS
Site in New Hampshire, USA where in 1944 an international conference was held to work out rules for a post-war international monetary system. It resulted in the creation of the International Monetary Fund and the World Bank. The system was based on fixed exchange rates combined with temporary financing facilities to overcome crises. Devaluation was only allowed in the case of a fundamental disequilibrium in a country's balance of payments.

BRIDGE FINANCING
Interim financing.

BRITISH THERMAL UNIT (BTU)
Heat needed to raise one pound of air-free water from 60 degrees Fahrenheit to 61 degrees at a constant pressure of one atmosphere.

BROAD TAPE
US term for news wires carrying prices and background information on securities and commodities as opposed to the narrower tape used by the exchanges.

BROADCAST
System of syndicating Eurocredits by offering widespread participation by telex/letter to potential lending institutions.

Br

BROKEN PERIOD
Forward foreign exchange deal for a non-standard period. Standard periods are, for example, one, two, three, six and twelve months.

BROKEN STOWAGE
Cargo space lost due to packages of uneven shape. Shipping term.

BROKER
Accredited buying/selling agent of securities or foreign exchange, a middleman/dealer in commodity transactions. In the money market and foreign exchange market he matches bids and offers, but does not sell or buy on his own account.

BROKERAGE
Fee or commission charged by a broker.

BROKER'S LINE
Direct telephone line between broker's office and a bank's dealing room.

BRUSSELS TARIFF NOMENCLATURE
Uniform method of classifying goods for customs purposes.

BSFF
See BUFFER STOCK FINANCING FACILITY.

BTU
See BRITISH THERMAL UNIT.

BUCKET SHOP
Unlawful or doubtful organisation dealing unscrupulously in commodities or stocks.

BUDGET
Official or governmental statement of actual or projected revenue and expenditure. Can also apply to corporate financial planning.

Bu

BUFFER STOCK
Stock of commodities held by an international association to stabilise prices and supplies by buying and selling using the stockpile's resources.

BUFFER STOCK FINANCING FACILITY (BSFF)
Facility which can be used by IMF member countries in balance of payments difficulties to draw up to 50 per cent of their IMF quota to finance contributions to international buffer stock arrangements. See IMF, QUOTA.

BUILDING SOCIETY
British institution which accepts deposits, pays interest on them and grants loans for house purchases secured by mortgages. In the US, Savings and Loan Associations.

BULGE
Rapid rise in prices.

BULK CARGO
Single category of cargo carried in bulk. Shipping term.

BULL
Investor who buys in the expectation of a rise in prices of the value of a stock, commodity or currency.

BULL MARKET
Rising market, or a market in which further price increases are expected due to strong demand.

BULLET BOND
Bond, usually a Eurobond, which has no early redemption, i.e. is redeemed at full maturity.

BULLION
Gold, silver or other precious metals in non-coined form.

BUNKER 'C'
Heavy residual fuel oil used by ships, industry and for large scale heating installations.

Bu

BUNKER FUEL
Any fuel oil or diesel fuel used by ships.

BUOYANT
Description of a market where prices rise easily with under-lying strong tone.

BUSINESS CYCLE
Alternative expansion and contraction or acceleration and deceleration in overall business activity shown by fluctuations in the economic aggregates.

BUSTED CONVERTIBLE
US term for a convertible issue which is virtually worthless, as the value of the supporting stock has fallen sharply.

BUY AT BEST
To bid higher and higher prices without any limit until the required quantity is purchased.

BUY BACK
See REPURCHASE AGREEMENT.

BUY BACK PRICE
Purchase price an oil company pays to a country for oil that the company produces but which belongs to the country.

BUY ON CLOSE
US term for purchases at the end of the trading session within the closing range.

BUY ON OPENING
US term for purchases at the start of the trading session within the opening range.

BUYER CREDIT
Export financing arrangement under which a foreign buyer raises a loan from a bank to pay an exporter.

BUYER'S MARKET
One in which producers are willing to produce, or sellers

willing to market, larger amounts than buyers are currently willing to buy at existing prices. This usually results in marked price declines.

BUYER'S OPTION

Allows a buyer to settle a forward contract at his option within a set period. He can decide between a choice of delivery dates or commodities of the same grade from different origins.

BUYER'S OVER

Price which is still valid after trading ends.

BUYER'S PREMIUM

Government payment to the EC purchaser of community products intended to encourage EC manufacturers to use domestic rather than non-EC products.

BUYING IN

If a seller of stocks fails to deliver them within the set time, the buyer may buy them in where he can and any additional costs and expenses are chargeable to the seller.

BUYING RATE

Rate at which a dealer or the principal market maker is willing to buy foreign currency.

BY-PRODUCT

Incidental yield of a production process.

CABLE

Foreign exchange market term for the dollar/sterling spot exchange rate.

CABLE TRANSFER

Transfer of money by cable between two centres.

C AND F

Cost and freight. Includes both the cost of the goods and freight charges. Shipping term.

Ca

CALENDAR
Timetable or schedule, official or otherwise, of future new securities issues on domestic and international capital markets.

CALL
Trading period during which the price for each future contract is established, i.e. opening, midsession or closing calls.

CALL FEATURE
Option on the part of the issuer in the US to redeem a bond issue prior to maturity at a pre-determined price.

CALL LOAN
Commercial bank loan payable on demand by the lender and repayable at any time by the borrower.

CALL LOAN RATE
See CALL RATE.

CALL MONEY
Interest bearing deposits which are repayable at call, i.e. on demand. Covers both domestic money market and Euromarket funds. Also known as day to day money or demand money.

CALL OPTION
Option or contract giving the holder the right to buy a certain amount of stock or commodity futures at a specified price at a specific forward date, or within a specified period.

CALL PRICE
Price at which a US bond issue can be called, usually at par or at a slight premium.

CALL RATE
Rate of interest payable on call money.

CALL RULE

Official bid price established competitively at the close of each day's trading and valid until the exchange reopens.

CALLABLE BOND

Bond which can be redeemed before maturity by the payment of a specified call price. This can help the borrower in cases when interest rates have fallen since the bond offering.

CALLABLE CAPITAL

Unpaid up part of a company's capital which can be called for payment to be made.

CALORIFIC VALUE

Measure of the amount of energy that is released in the form of heat when a fuel is burned, often expressed in BTUs.

CAMBISTE

Foreign exchange dealer.

CAP

See COMMON AGRICULTURAL POLICY.

CAPACITY UTILISATION

Ratio of output compared to the full capacity of a company, industrial sector or economy. A key to the level of economic activity.

CAPITAL

Equity of a company representing net worth in the form of issued stock at book value and retained net earnings.

CAPITAL ACCOUNT

(a) Balance of payment items not included in the current account, including investment and deposit funds, aid and military expenditure.

(b) Also used in US accounting to indicate the amount of equity in a business.

Ca

CAPITAL ALLOWANCES
Allowances against tax on expenditure on capital equipment used by industry or business.

CAPITAL EMPLOYED
Capital used in a business. It may refer to net assets, but often includes bank loans and overdrafts.

CAPITAL EXPORTS
Outflow of capital account funds. If substantial over a very short period, it is a capital flight.

CAPITAL FORMATION
Net addition to capital stock in a given period.

CAPITAL GAIN
Increase in the value of a capital asset when it is sold or transferred, compared to its initial worth. Inflation and currency movements can affect the 'real' capital gain. Capital loss is the opposite.

CAPITAL GEARING
Relationship between the different types of capital used by a company. See GEARING.

CAPITAL GOODS
Typically fixed assets such as plant or machinery used in the manufacture of other goods. Also called capital equipment.

CAPITAL INTENSIVE
Use of relatively large amounts of capital to raise production, instead of increasing the contribution of other inputs, e.g. the labour force or raw materials.

CAPITAL INVESTMENT
Investment by a government or a company in capital goods.

CAPITAL MARKET
Market for loanable funds. Covers medium and long term

finance while the money market is more involved with short term finance. Both are closely inter-related.

CAPITALISATION
Total market value of a company's issued shares, the amount of a company's capital, as well as its composition, i.e. debt, equity.

CAR OR CARLOAD
Term used in US commodity trading for the load of a railway freight wagon or car. Now refers to one commodities contract.

CARAT
Measure of the fineness of gold. Pure gold is 24 carats, i.e. there is no alloy. Thus 19 carat gold represents 19 parts gold and five parts alloy. It is also used as a measure of weight for precious stones.

CARBON BLACK
Substantially pure form of finely divided carbon based on liquid or gaseous hydrocarbons, used in making rubber products and inks.

CARRIAGE
Cost and manner of conveying goods.

CARRIES
A London Metal Exchange term for the simultaneous matching purchase of one delivery with the sale of another. In other markets called STRADDLES or SWITCHES.

CARRY
Cost of financing, i.e. borrowing to purchase, a position in financial instruments. When the short term interest rate is greater than the current return on the instrument, the carry is a negative one. If the financing cost is less than the return, it is a positive carry.

CARRYING CHARGE
(a) Cost of storing a physical commodity including insurance, storage and interest charges.

(b) Full carrying charge market. A situation in the futures market when price differentials between delivery months fully reflect insurance, storage and interest costs.

CARRYOVER
(a) Part of current crop production carried over into the next crop year, or that part of current supplies of a commodity comprising stocks from the previous year's production.
(b) Carrying over the settlement of account on the stock exchange until the next account period, by the payment of interest.

CARRYOVER DAY
UK stock exchange term for the settlement day which starts each new trading account of approximately two weeks duration.

CASH COMMODITY
Physical commodity as distinct from a futures commodity.

CASH DELIVERY
Same day delivery in US securities markets.

CASH FLOW
Sum of pre-tax profits and depreciation allowances. See NET CASH FLOW.

CASH MANAGEMENT BILL
Very short term US Treasury Bills with one to twenty days maturity and designed to maintain balances until taxes are received.

CASH MARKET
Spot market in commodity trading. In the US, cash grains cover both spot and forward deliveries.

CASH RATIO
Ratio of cash and related assets to liabilities; in the case of a bank, the ratio of cash to total deposit liabilities.

CASING
Steel pipe cemented into a well to prevent the sides from collapsing and to block unwanted fluids entering the well from the surrounding rock. Oil term.

CATALYST
Substance aiding or promoting a chemical reaction but remaining chemically unchanged after the reaction.

CBOE
Chicago Board Options Exchange.

CBOT
Chicago Board of Trade.

CBT
Clean ballast tanker. Shipping term.

CCC
Commodity Credit Corporation. US government agency, set up in 1933, responsible for directing and financing major US Department of Agriculture action programmes including price support and production adjustment. It also directs and finances agricultural export activities, including credit sales, barter deals, export payments and foreign food aid.

CCT
Common Community Tariff, as applied by the EC. The CCT code is a numerical and alphabetical codification of goods to permit their identification in the internal and external trade of the EC.

CDR
See CONTINENTAL DEPOSITARY RECEIPT.

CEDEL
Centrale de Livraison de Valeurs Mobilières, Luxembourg. A computerised clearing system for Eurobonds.

CENTRAL BANK
Major regulatory bank in a nation's monetary system, generally government controlled. Its role normally includes control of

Ce

the credit system, the note issue, supervision of commercial banks, management of exchange reserves and the national currency's value as well as acting as the government's banker.

CENTRAL GOVERNMENT BORROWING REQUIREMENT (CGBR)

Difference in the UK between the government's expenditure and revenue excluding the local authority sector. When it includes the local authority sector, it becomes the public sector borrowing requirement. See PSBR.

CENTRAL RATE

Exchange rate against the European Currency Unit (ECU) adopted for each currency within the European Monetary System. Central rates are used to tie members' currencies together in a grid of fixed parities. Similar parities are calculated via the ECU central rate between all member states' national currencies. See EUROPEAN CURRENCY UNIT.

CEREALS

Edible grains. These are wheat, oats, barley, rye, rice, maize (corn), millet and sorghum.

CERTIFICATE OF DEPOSIT (CD)

Interest bearing negotiable time deposit of fixed maturity at a commercial bank. The posted rate is an indicated rate at which the bank is willing to take on the deposit. However, a bank will negotiate a rate with a large depositor. US banks can only negotiate rates of CDs of $100,000 or more, or with maturities over four years.

CERTIFICATE OF ORIGIN

Establishes the country of origin for imported goods. It enables the customs authorities to determine whether the goods can benefit from preferential tariff rates due to their country of origin. Issued by Chambers of Commerce and similar bodies.

CERTIFICATED (OR CERTIFIED) STOCKS

Stocks which have been inspected and approved as deliverable quality against futures contracts. In grains, stocks in deliverable position.

CFA FRANC

Communauté Française Africaine franc used mainly in former French West African colonies. It has a fixed parity against the French franc.

CFP FRANC

French Pacific Community franc used in departments and overseas territories in the Pacific.

CFTC

Commodity Futures Trading Commission. Established by the US Congress to administer the 1974 Commodity Futures Trading Act. It has jurisdiction over all commodities contract markets in the US. It comprises five commissioners, one of whom is designated chairman. All are appointed by the President. They are subject to Senate confirmation and independent of all government departments.

CHARGE ACCOUNT

US term for credit account.

CHARTERPARTY

Contract under which the charterer has the use of the ship for the carriage of goods for a voyage or a certain time. Such a contract may also act as security for a loan to the shipowner from a bank. The money paid to the owner is known as freight.

CHARTERING AGENT

Specialised broker engaged in finding cargo space. Shipping term.

CHARTERPARTY ASSIGNMENT

Legal agreement under which the sum paid by the charterer to the shipowner is assigned to a bank as security for a loan to the owner, often for the construction of a vessel.

CHARTING

Use of graphs and charts by a chartist in the technical analysis of markets to plot and forecast trends. Price movements and average price movements are often part of charting.

Ch

CHICAGO BOARD OF TRADE
A major commodity futures exchange specialising in grains, soybeans and soybean products. It also trades in plywood, silver, gold and financial futures.

CHICAGO SCHOOL
Free market philosophy school of monetarists, centred on the University of Chicago and associated with Professor Milton Friedman.

CHIPS
Clearing House Interbank Payment System. A computerised clearing system in New York bringing together members of the New York Clearing House and others.

CHOPT
Charterer's option. Shipping term.

CHRISTMAS TREE
Assembly of pipes and valves attached to a production well-head controlling the flow of oil or gas and stopping a possible blowout.

CICILS
Confédération Internationale du Commerce et des Industries des Légumes Secs (the International Confederation of Pulse Trade and Industry) based in Paris.

CIF
Cost, insurance and freight. A CIF price means that it includes the cost of goods, their insurance and freight. The purchaser of CIF goods bears no expenses until he takes the goods from the ship or plane at destination. Due fulfilment by the seller may take place when he passes to the buyer the invoice, the insurance policy and bill of lading.

CLASS, WHEAT
There are five official basic classes of US wheat: Hard Red Spring, Hard Red Winter, Durum, Soft Red Winter and White.

CLAUSED BILL OF EXCHANGE
Bill of exchange specifying certain conditions involved in completing the bill.

CLEAN
(a) Bill of lading free from endorsement or clause suggesting damage to the goods carried.
(b) Bill of exchange free of any other documents.

CLEAN (WHITE)
Highly refined oil products, such as aviation spirit, motor spirit, kerosene and some grades of gas oil.

CLEAN FLOAT
Flotation of a currency on foreign exchange markets without official intervention.

CLEAN OIL
Refined oil.

CLEAN OIL VESSEL
Ship employed in carrying refined products such as aviation spirit, motor spirit, kerosene and some grades of gas oil.

CLEARANCE
(a) Trades cleared by a clearing house.
(b) Volume of goods cleared through a port.

CLEARING
(a) Procedure through which a clearing house or association becomes buyer to each seller of a futures contract, and seller to each buyer, and assumes responsibility for protecting buyers and sellers from financial loss by assuring performance on each contract.
(b) National system for clearing cheques.

CLEARING BANK
Member bank of a national cheque clearing system.

Cl

CLEARING HOUSE
Adjunct to commodity/stock exchanges through which transactions executed on the floor are settled. Also charged with assuring the proper conduct of delivery procedures and the adequate financing of the trading.

CLEARING HOUSE FUNDS
Payments made through a computerised clearing system. See CHIPS.

CLEARING MEMBER
Firm which is a member of a clearing house organisation. All clearing members must be exchange members, though not all exchange members need to belong to the clearing house.

CLEARING PRICE
Daily price at which a clearing house clears all trades and settles all contracts between members for each contract month. See SETTLEMENT PRICE.

CLLG
Shipping term for cancelling.

CLOSE
End of a trading session when last orders are executed.

CLOSE COMPANY
UK term for a company controlled by five or fewer persons whether directors or otherwise. The US equivalent is the closed company.

CLOSED ECONOMY
In theory an economy completely closed to international trade with no exports, imports or capital movements. In practice where trade and capital movements are severely restricted.

CLOSED END (INVESTMENT) COMPANY

Investment company with a fixed capital structure, with a number of fixed shares outstanding which are traded in the secondary market and cannot be redeemed or increased.

CLOSED POSITION

Opening transaction in commodities matched by a corresponding offsetting trade in the same delivery—a purchase matched by a later sale or vice versa.

CLOSING OUT

Action offsetting a long or short position.

CLOSING PRICE

Price or price range recorded by an exchange during or at the close of a trading session.

CLUB

General distribution of tasks within a group of banks involved in loan syndication on the Euromarkets. It eschews the traditional system of designating lead managers, co-managers etc. May also refer to governmental arrangements for rescheduling debt.

CMEA

Council for Mutual Economic Assistance (Comecon) established in 1949 with headquarters in Moscow to co-ordinate the economic development of member countries. It comprises Bulgaria, Cuba, Czechoslovakia, German Democratic Republic, Hungary, Mongolia, Poland, Romania, Vietnam and the USSR. Albania is a non-active member.

COA

See AFFREIGHTMENT. Shipping term.

COAL EQUIVALENT

Used in energy consumption statistics as an overall measure.

Co

COAL (HYDROGENATED)
Production of artificial mineral oil from coal by combining the carbon in coal with hydrogen to form hydrocarbons.

COCERAL
Comité du Commerce des Céréales et des Aliments du Bétail de la CEE (Committee for Trade in Cereals and Animal Feed in the EC).

COEFFICIENTS OF EQUIVALENCE
Used in calculating daily levies on grain imported into the EC. The EC official prices relate to grain of a standard EC quality and the quoted values of grain offered are adjusted according to quality by the addition or subtraction of these co-efficients of equivalence.

COFFEE RUST
Serious fungus disease attacking coffee plants resulting in the plant losing its leaves, thus reducing the coffee yield. After a number of years, the affected plants die.

CO-FINANCING
Finance jointly provided for a country by commercial banks and international financing institutions, such as the IMF, World Bank or regional development banks. It is one way of effectively increasing the amount lent by international institutions. The terms they insist on for ensuring the loan conditions are observed, reassure commercial banks concerned over the possible security of their own loans. The banks are thus more willing to lend.

COGECA
Comité Generale de la Coopération Agricole des Pays de la Communauté (General Committee for Agricultural Co-operation in the EC).

COINCIDENT INDICATOR
Measure of economic activity such as unemployment or industrial production which moves in the same direction and at the same time as total economic activity.

48

COLLATERAL
Property or securities pledged to secure a loan, sometimes subject to central bank margin limits.

CO-MANAGER
In securities issues, usually an invitee on an ad hoc basis either by the lead manager or at the request of the issuer of the securities or guarantor. Usually between two and ten co-managers share responsibility, chiefly for pricing and placement. As a rule co-managers make larger underwriting commitments than do syndicate participants.

COMBO
Combined carrier. Vessel able to carry ore, oil or bulk cargoes. Shipping term.

COMECON
See CMEA

COMEX
New York Commodity Exchange Inc.

COMMERCIAL BANK
Bank concentrating principally on short term industrial and commercial lending. Typically such an institution will offer a broad range of services to business and consumers, including current (checking) accounts, commercial, consumer and mortgage loans.

COMMERCIAL FIELD
Oil and/or gas field able to generate sufficient income to make it worth developing.

COMMERCIAL PAPER
Promissory note or draft of a corporation, government agency or bank holding company, usually unsecured but backed by unused bank credit lines and issued for short term credit needs. It normally has a maturity of up to 270 days. Commercial paper is usually sold at a discount from face value. Directly placed paper is sold by the issuer directly to the

investor while dealer placed paper is sold to an intermediary who in turn reoffers it to investors. Many companies have the capability to sell directly and there is a slight yield advantage in directly placing the paper.

COMMERCIAL TRANSACTION
Foreign exchange deal with non-bank party.

COMMISSION
Pro rata remuneration for work done as an agent. Brokerage charged according to an official minimum scale laid down by an exchange. In the US, however, rates are negotiated rather than tied to a fixed scale.

COMMISSION HOUSE
Concern that buys and sells actual commodities or futures contracts for the accounts of customers, i.e. its income is generated by the commission charged for its service. In the US, exchange fixed securities commissions were abolished in 1975. Since then, scales have been set on an individual basis.

COMMITMENT FEE
Fee charged by banks on the unused portion of a loan.

COMMODITY CREDIT CORPORATION
See CCC.

COMMODITY EXCHANGE
Market in which commodity futures are bought and sold. Major commodity exchanges are found in London, Chicago, New York, Paris, Sydney, Hong Kong, Kuala Lumpur, Tokyo, Osaka and New Orleans. Delivery of the underlying commodity may also take place.

COMMODITY STABILISATION AGREEMENTS
International agreements involving producers, and in some cases consumers, in efforts to stabilise production and/or prices of commodities.

COMMON AGRICULTURAL POLICY
Operated by the EC and based on target prices and variable import levies. Also covers structural improvement of agriculture in the EC.

COMMON MARKET
Europe Communities (see EC).

COMMON STOCK
US equivalent of ordinary shares. See ORDINARY CAPITAL.

COMPENSATION BALANCE
Amount of a commercial loan, usually expressed as a percentage of the loan which the borrower is required to keep on deposit with the bank.

COMPENSATION TRADE
System under which an exporter accepts that part of the purchase price is paid for by goods from the importing country.

COMPENSATORY FINANCING
IMF facility providing short term finance to compensate for fluctuations in a country's export levels caused by circumstances largely outside a country's control.

COMPETITIVE DEVALUATION
Devaluation designed to gain a competitive advantage in export markets.

COMPETITIVE TRADER
Member of the New York Stock Exchange trading in stocks for an account in which he has an interest.

COMPOSITE INDEX
Average or combined index of dissimilar component series. The US Department of Commerce, for example, issues a closely followed composite index of 12 leading economic

indicators. The NYSE composite index of some 1500 common stocks includes four subsectors—industrials, transportation, utilities, finance.

COMPTROLLER OF THE CURRENCY

US Treasury Department official responsible for chartering national banks and with primary supervisory authority over them. All national banks must be members of the Federal Reserve system, and are insured by the Federal Deposit Insurance Corporation.

COMPUTER TRADING

US trading groups which trade commodity futures on the basis of computer produced buy/sell indicators.

CONDENSATE

Gaseous hydrocarbons which condense as they are extracted from a well.

CONDENSER

Equipment which changes a material from a vapour to a liquid state. Oil term.

CONDITIONALITY

Conditions imposed when a country draws funds from the IMF related to its credit tranches. There are four tranches and borrowing under each tranche attracts its own conditions. Other conditions apply to borrowing beyond regular credit tranches such as where a country borrows to replace finance lost through a decline in exports—see COMPENSATORY FINANCING.

CONFERENCE LINES

Association of shipowning lines which operate on a given route. Standard tariff rates are fixed and a regular service operated for the mutual benefit of both the merchant trading in that area and the shipowner who runs his line.

CONGESTED MARKET

Market in which one or more individuals or groups hold

concentrated positions, raising the possibility that contracts may not liquidate in an orderly fashion.

CONGLOMERATE
Corporation with widely diversified interests, normally built up by acquisition.

CONSECUTIVES
Specific number of voyages performed by a vessel consecutively on a single voyage basis for the account of one charterer.

CONSIGNMENT
Goods shipped by a producer or dealer to an agent on the understanding they will be sold at the best possible price or properly looked after. The shipper retains ownership.

CONSOLIDATED ANNUITIES (CONSOLS)
British government securities first consolidated into a single stock in 1751. No redeemable date.

CONSOLIDATED BALANCE SHEET
Shows the financial situation of a corporation and its subsidiaries.

CONSOLIDATED FUND
Funds in the UK standing to the account of the Exchequer into which revenue is paid from taxation and which is used to finance government expenditure.

CONSOLIDATED TAPE
Tape which since 1975 has reported transactions in listed securities on the NYSE, AMEX and regional stock exchanges.

CONSOLIDATION
(a) Taking of profits which have been made on speculative shares and reinvesting the proceeds in more conservative stocks.

(b) Substitution of national currencies held in a country's exchange reserves by a new international monetary asset. e.g. SDRs.

(c) Accounting method used in presenting financial statements.

(d) US term for a combination or fusion of two or more companies into a new company.

CONSORTIUM BANK

Specialised bank with a group of other banks as shareholders but where no single bank holds a majority of the equity. Usually involved in large scale international financing operations via the Euromarkets.

CONSUMER PRICE INDEX

Monthly index measuring the changes in cost of a basket of consumer essentials—food, rent, mortgages, clothing, heating, fuel, travel etc. A major indicator of a nation's inflation rate.

CONSUMER SPENDING

Expenditure on goods and service for immediate consumption by households and an indicator of the level of economic activity.

CONTANGO

(a) Charge made by a stockbroker in the UK for carrying over a position from one account to another without paying for or delivering the stock.

(b) Commodity, e.g. London Metal Exchange term used when prices for near dates or months are quoted at a discount to later deliveries.

CONTANGO DAY

On the London stock market it refers to the last dealing day of the account, i.e. the day on which the contango is arranged.

CONTINENTAL DEPOSITARY RECEIPT (CDR)

Bearer document allowing trading to take place in US, UK

and Japanese registered company shares on certain European exchanges.

CONTRACT
(a) Agreement between two or more parties intended to be legally enforceable.
(b) On commodity markets the precise specifications, e.g. price, delivery point and delivery date laid down by a futures market to denote a standard trading unit.

CONTRACT FINANCING
Finance for projects which use a commercial contract as security.

CONTRACT GRADES (UNITS)
Standard set for each commodity which must be observed when commodities are delivered against futures contracts. Most contracts have a number of grades or qualities which result in a premium or discount when delivery actually takes place.

CONTRACT MONTH
Month in which delivery is due under a futures contract, i.e. when the contract matures.

CONTRACT TRADING VOLUME
Total number of contracts traded in a commodity or a commodity delivery month during a specific period.

CONVERSION PREMIUM
Premium paid to redeem outstanding bonds before maturity.

CONVERTIBILITY
(a) Monetary term loosely used to describe exchangeability of a currency into gold or SDRs. More properly, it refers to the free and uncontrolled exchangeability of one currency into another.
(b) In the US bond market, an attribute of some bonds that

makes them convertible into the common stock of the same company at a price usually set above the current market level.

CONVERTIBLE BOND/DEBENTURE

Corporate loan stock that can be converted into the issuer's common (ordinary) or preferred stock at a stipulated price over a designated time period.

COP

Custom of port. Relates to customs and practices which have gradually been established for movements in a port, usually concerning loading and discharge. Shipping term.

COPA

Comité des Organisations Professionnelles Agricoles de la Communauté (the Committee for Professional Agricultural Organisations in the EC) i.e. federation of EC farm unions.

COREPER

Committee of Permanent Representatives which groups the member states' 'ambassadors' to the EC. It reviews and negotiates draft legislation before decisions by the Council of Ministers.

CORNER

To acquire control of the supply of a commodity or security so that it becomes possible to manipulate its price by cornering the market. Increasingly prohibited by exchange rules and legislations.

CORRECTIVES

When EC export refunds for farm products are prefixed, correctives may be applied to adjust the current value to reflect the prevailing circumstances in forward markets. These may be added to or deducted from export restitutions.

CORRESPONDENT

Bank or financial organisation which acts on behalf of a similar organisation in a centre where the latter is not physically represented.

CORSET

Limitation on the growth of bank lending in the UK where banks had to deposit funds with the Bank of England without benefit of interest if the limit was exceeded. The corset was abandoned in 1980.

COST OF LIVING INDEX

Roughly equivalent to, though often broader than, CONSUMER or RETAIL PRICE INDEX.

COST PUSH INFLATION

When excessive wage rises push up manufacturing costs resulting in higher prices, which in turn stimulate further wage rises. Opposite to demand-pull.

COTTON GIN

Machinery separating the cottonseed and foreign materials from cotton fibres.

COTTONSEED OIL, MEAL

Oil is extracted from the cottonseed by crushing. The residue becomes cottonseed meal and is used as animal feed.

COUNTERVAILING DUTY

Import duty imposed over and above normal levels when an importing country considers the export price to contain a subsidy.

COUNTRY RISK

Risk of lending funds to or making an investment in a particular country.

COUPON

Interest rate payable on bearer, and sometimes registered, securities especially bonds. It also means the detachable certificate entitling the bearer to payment of the interest.

COVER

(a) Collateral deposited as security against an open position or borrowing.

Co

(b) Forward contract to protect against foreign exchange rate fluctuations.

(c) On commodity markets the purchase of futures to offset a previously established short position.

(d) Extent to which a company's dividend and/or interest disbursement is matched or exceeded by its earnings.

(e) Import cover whereby gold and foreign exchange reserves represent in sum the value of imports for one, two, three or more months.

COVERED INTEREST ARBITRAGE

Borrowing a currency followed by conversion into a second currency for investment, then selling the second currency for future delivery against the first currency.

CPI

See CONSUMER PRICE INDEX.

CQS

Consolidated Quotation System. A US system which electronically collects and disseminates current bids and asking quotations, with size, from and to all market centres in which listed stocks are traded.

CRACKING

Production process in the petroleum industry whereby feedstock is subjected to a high temperature for a limited period in order to boost the output of light products at the expense of heavier types of fuel.

CRACKING (CATALYTIC)

Cracking process in which a catalyst is used to promote reaction. It allows cracking to take place at a lower temperature.

CRAWLING PEG

Technique to allow exchange rates slowly but steadily to appreciate/depreciate, either automatically or with deliberate guidance.

CREDIT RATING

Overall credit worthiness of a borrower. In the US the two rating agencies are Moody's and Standard & Poor's. A top rating is described as 'triple A' or 'AAA'.

CREDIT RISK

Risk that a borrower may default on his obligations; a danger that repayment will not take place.

CREDIT UNIONS

Financial co-operation organisations in the US comprising individuals with a common affiliation, e.g. employer, neighbourhood. They accept members' deposits in the form of share purchases, pay interest out of earnings while providing consumer instalment credit for their members.

CREDITOR NATION

Country with a balance of payments surplus.

CROP YEAR

Time period from the start of one harvest to the next, varying according to the commodity and country. e.g. 1 June to 31 May for US wheat, 1 September to 31 August for US soybeans.

CROSS CURRENCY EXPOSURE

Where a corporation's debt service needs in a given currency are not covered by revenue, or potential revenue, in that currency.

CROSS DEFAULT

Clause in a loan agreement stipulating that default by borrower on any other loans will be regarded as a default on the loan governed by that clause.

CROSS RATE

Exchange rate relationship between two currencies based on each other's relationship with a third, typically the US dollar.

Cr

CRUDE (EQUITY)
Oil belonging to companies on which the tax and royalty payments are made.

CRUDE OIL
Oil produced from a reservoir after any associated gas has been removed. Also known as crude.

CRUDE (PARTICIPATION)
Oil belonging to the host government in proportion to its stake in the company. Mainly sold for distribution by the companies at a 'buy-back' price.

CRUSH MARGIN
Value of oil and meal produced from crushing oilseeds compared with its cost.

CULPEPER SWITCH
Federal Reserve central message switching facility at Culpeper, Virginia, US, used to transmit messages electronically between Federal Reserve districts on the Fedwire. Billions of dollars of funds and securities are thus handled daily.

CUM ALL
Including all supplementary advantages attached to a share.

CUM CAPITALISATION (CUM NEW)
The share price including free shares issued to shareholders under a capitalisation issue.

CUM COUPON
The situation where the purchaser of a bond is entitled to receive the next interest payment.

CUM DIVIDEND
The situation where a UK stock being sold includes the rights to the next dividend. Share prices become ex div, i.e. without rights to the dividend, a short time before the dividend is due for payment.

Cu

CUM RIGHTS
Shares sold which include any rights attached to them.

CUMULATIVE
Stock or share, generally preference or preferred, the owner-ship of which carries an entitlement to receive dividend arrears before payment out of current profits is made on stock and ordinary shares, not carrying this entitlement.

CURRENCY AVAILABILITY
Agreement allowing lending to take place in a currency other than that intended due to its non-availability.

CURRENCY BAND
Margin within which a currency is permitted to move.

CURRENCY BASKET
Cocktail of currencies individually weighted and whose com-bined value is the equivalent of one unit. See ECU.

CURRENCY CLAUSE
Used in contracts to set a fixed rate between two currencies, to avoid the impact of devaluation or revaluation.

CURRENCY EXCHANGE
Arrangement whereby two companies in different countries agree to cover specific foreign exchange needs by matching loans in their national currencies. It does not require an exchange of currency between the two countries.

CURRENCY OPTION CLAUSE
Allows payment of principal and interest on a Eurobond issued in one currency to be made in a different currency at the option of the purchaser.

CURRENT ACCOUNT
Balance of payments embracing a country's trade account and international transactions in invisible goods or services.

Cu

CURRENT ASSETS
Corporate assets which can be realised reasonably quickly. These include debtors, stock in trade, work in progress, bank balances, marketable securities. In the US it can be defined as cash, US government bonds, receivables, monies usually due within one year and inventories.

CURRENT LIABILITIES
Counterpart of current assets, representing reasonably short term working commitments of a company. These include trade creditors, sums due to banks, taxation payable and declared dividends.

CURRENT LIQUIDITY RATIO
Current liabilities minus liquid (current) assets divided by profit or cash flow multiplied by 365 (days).

CURRENT RATIO
Balance sheet ratio of current assets over current liabilities. The difference between the two is net working capital which provides a guide to the company's level of liquidity.

CURRENT YIELD
(a) In the UK a flat or running yield (as opposed to a redemption yield). It is the annual return which an investor would secure by investing £100 at the current price in a security paying a known dividend. It is calculated by multiplying the annual dividend rate percent by the nominal value of the security and dividing by the price, the last two items being of the same denomination. It takes no account of the profit or loss, if any, on redemption, nor of the tax payable by the investor.
(b) In the US, the percentage return obtained by dividing current dollar income by the market price of the stock or bond.

CUSTOMS DUTY
Border tax usually levied on imports.

Dc

CUSTOMS UNION
Agreement by a group of countries to abolish internal tariffs and adopt a uniform or common external tariff.

DATED DATE
Date from which interest begins to accrue on a new US bond issue.

DATED SECURITIES
Securities with a fixed redemption date. 'Long dated securities' indicates redemption is a long way off.

DAWN RAID
UK term for the acquisition of shares at a price which results in the purchase of a large block of equity in a company in a short space of time. Such acquisition is now limited in London except under prescribed conditions. Purchases often took place at the start of trading.

DAY ORDER
Commodity order given for one day at a specific price. If it cannot be executed, it is automatically cancelled.

DAY TRADERS
Traders who acquire and liquidate the same futures position during one trading day. In the US also known as 'scalpers'.

DAYLIGHT EXPOSURE LIMIT
Limits on a bank's foreign exchange business during a working day either overall or by currency.

DAYS PURPOSE
Number of days required by a ship for loading and unloading purposes.

DCE
Domestic Credit Expansion. In the UK the PUBLIC

Dc

SECTOR BORROWING REQUIREMENT (PSBR) minus sales of public sector debt to the non-bank private sector plus the increase in bank lending to the private and overseas sectors.

DCF
See DISCOUNTED CASH FLOW

DEAD FREIGHT
Paid when a charterer does not provide a full cargo, and the shipowner charges freight for the space which would have been used.

DEAD RENT
In mining leases rent which is payable whether a mine is worked or not.

DEADWEIGHT
Weight which a vessel is capable of carrying by way of cargo, plus bunkers, stores and fresh water, when loading to the maximum permitted marks. It is measured in tons of 2,240 lbs.

DEALER
Trader in securities, commodities or foreign exchange.

DEALER LOAN
Overnight loan to a dealer, backed by collateral.

DEALING FOR NEW TIME
On the London Stock Exchange purchase or sale of securities for the new account during the last two days of the previous account.

DEALING WITHIN THE ACCOUNT
Purchase and sale of shares within the same account.

DEAR MONEY
When the cost of funds produces a constricted borrowing environment.

De

DEBENTURE
A written acknowledgement of a debt; a bond. In the US a debenture whether straight or convertible is secured by a general guarantee and not by a lien on specific assets, while bonds are unsecured. In the UK a debenture is usually secured by a charge on corporate assets, while bonds are unsecured.

DEBT MANAGEMENT
Manipulation of three aspects of government debt: the level of interest rates, the pattern of ownership and the maturity schedule.

DEBT SERVICE RATIO (REQUIREMENT)
(a) Cost to a country of servicing its foreign debts and, in particular, debts owed by the public sector and publicly guaranteed debt. This cost comprises the total of interest payments and repayments of principal as a percentage of export earnings. A level of 20 per cent is normally considered an acceptable maximum, but accurately establishing the exact figure is often difficult.
(b) Can also apply to the debt servicing needs of a corporation.

DEBTOR NATION
Country with a balance of payments deficit, the opposite of CREDITOR NATION.

DECLARATION DATE
Last date for declaring an option. See OPTION.

DEED OF ARRANGEMENT
In the UK, arrangement made between a debtor and creditor to try to avoid bankruptcy or liquidation.

DEED OF TRANSFER
Document authorising a company to transfer stock from one shareholder to another.

DEFAULT
(a) If a borrower does not repay either the interest or the principal according to the conditions governing the loan, he

De

is in default. In certain cases the creditors may consent to a rescheduling of the payments to avoid default.
(b) Failure of a party under a futures contract to fulfill the contract requirements or failure to make or take delivery of the physical commodity in a futures market.

DEFENSIVE STOCKS
Shares with a high yield, low price earnings ratio and modest prospect for price appreciation. Normally found in economic sectors less subject to cyclical fluctuations.

DEFERRED DELIVERIES
Distant months in futures trading.

DEFICIENCY PAYMENTS
System of supporting farm product prices used in the UK before it joined the EC. It involved payments to farmers of the difference between average free market prices for certain products, and guaranteed prices (normally higher) fixed annually.

DEFICIT
Shortfall (a) in balance of trade measuring net imports.
(b) In balance of payments measures net foreign payments and incurred liabilities.
(c) In a budget measures outlays net of revenues.

DEFICIT FINANCING
Budgetary policy which produces a deficit and hence a growing government borrowing requirement. It can be the direct result of positive governmental action or of a failure to control spending.

DEFLATION
Usually a depressive slowdown in the rise or fall of prices associated with a contraction in the supply of money and credit and accompanied by a decline in output and a rise in unemployment.

DEFLATOR
Difference between real and nominal Gross National Product, measuring the overall inflation rate in the economy. See GROSS NATIONAL PRODUCT.

DELIVERABLE GRADES
See CONTRACT GRADES.

DELIVERABLE STOCKS
See CERTIFICATED STOCKS.

DELIVERY (COMMODITIES)
Tender and receipt of the actual commodity or financial instrument, or in settlement of a futures contract.

DELIVERY MONTH
Month in which a futures contract matures and becomes deliverable.

DELIVERY NOTICE
Written notice from a clearing house of seller's intention to deliver the actual commodity against his open short futures position. Also known in the US as 'issues and stops'.

DELIVERY POINTS
Locations where stocks of commodities or financial instruments represented by futures contracts may be delivered in fulfilment of a contract. The commodity exchanges designate the specific locations.

DELIVERY PRICE
Settlement price set by a clearing house for deliveries of commodities against futures contracts.

DEMAND DEPOSIT
Bank deposit withdrawal that can be made without prior notice. Also called a sight deposit, a current account balance or checking account (US).

De

DEMAND LINE OF CREDIT
Line of credit with a bank which allows a client to borrow on demand.

DEMAND PULL
Also called demand-led inflation, classically defined as too much money chasing too few goods, opposite to COST-PUSH.

DEMISE CHARTER
Charter of a ship which transfers ownership of the vessel to the charterer for the duration.

DEMURRAGE
Extra charge made by the shipowner if a vessel takes more than the agreed time for loading and discharge.

DENATURED WHEAT
Wheat treated under the EC Common Agricultural Policy to make it unfit for human consumption. The intention is to stop it qualifying for a bread wheat subsidy.

DEPLETION ACCOUNTING
Accounting practice consisting of charges against earnings based upon the amount of an asset taken out of the total reserves of that asset, e.g. metals, oil or gas in a given accounting period.

DEPLETION CONTROL
Limits on the rate at which oil and gas or other mineral reserves can be used.

DEPOSIT CEILING RATES OF INTEREST
In the US the maximum interest rates payable on savings and time deposits at federally insured commercial banks, mutual savings banks, savings and loan associations and credit unions. Ceilings are set by the Federal Reserve Board, the Federal Deposit Insurance Corporation, the Federal Home Loan Bank Board and the National Credit Union Administration. Under existing legislation these ceilings will be phased out by 1986.

DEPOSITARY RECEIPT

Document indicating ownership of a commodity stored in a bank depository. Also called WAREHOUSE RECEIPT.

DEPRECIATION

Reduction in the book value of a corporate fixed asset over the asset's economic life, or reduction in the market value of a currency.

DEPTH OF MARKET

Extent of business which can be done in a market without causing a price disturbance. Reflects market liquidity. See THIN MARKET.

DERIVED FUEL

Form of energy manufactured from a primary fuel such as coal or oil, e.g. electricity, coke or town gas.

DERIVED TARGET PRICE

Basic EC target price for a particular farm product less the transport costs from the main deficit area to the area for which the derived target price is fixed.

DERV

Diesel Engine Road Vehicle fuel derived from gas oil.

DETERGENT

Cleansing liquid or solid, normally made from petroleum products.

DEVALUATION

Downward adjustment of a currency's official par value or central exchange rate.

DEVELOPMENT ASSISTANCE COMMITTEE (DAC)

OECD committee charged with promoting financial assistance for developing countries.

De

DEVELOPMENT PHASE
Period when a proven oil or gas field is brought into production by drilling production wells.

DEVELOPMENT WELL
Well used to produce oil or gas from a proven field.

DEVIATED WELL
Well not drilled vertically, used to reach different parts of a reservoir from a single platform.

DEVIATION
Conditions under which a ship under a marine insurance policy may deviate from its planned course.

DEXTROSE
Sugar substitute obtained from corn starch.

DIESEL FUEL
Light oil fuel used in diesel engines.

DIFFERENTIALS
Discounts or premiums permitted when delivering a commodity of different standard or at different location from that specified in the futures contract.

DIFFERENTIAL TARIFF
Tariff which gives preference to, or discriminates against, certain goods from a country or group of countries, or a mixture of both.

DILUTION
Reduction in per share participation in net earnings through an increase in issued stock.

DIRECT INVESTMENT
Corporate investment in the producer side of a foreign economy, as distinct from portfolio investment.

DIRECT PAPER

Commercial paper sold direct by the issuer to investors.

DIRECT PLACEMENT

Placing a new (corporate) issue directly, usually with institutional investors, rather than through an underwritten offering.

DIRECT QUOTATION

Foreign exchange quotation which expresses a foreign currency in terms of the domestic currency.

DIRECTIVES

Acts of the EC Council or Commission which are addressed to member states. The objectives are binding but the exact method of implementation is left to the individual states.

DIRTY BILL OF LADING

Bill of lading which qualifies the goods being carried. See FOUL BILL OF LADING.

DIRTY (BLACK)

Crude oils, fuel oil and some lower grades of oil.

DIRTY FLOAT

Floating currency when controlled by intervention of the authorities, i.e. not freely according to market conditions.

DIRTY OIL VESSELS

Vessels carrying crude oil, fuel and diesel oils and some grades of gas oil.

DISCHARGING

Disposal of goods, money or commodities held over a long period of time.

DISCOUNT

(a) In financial terms, the difference between present and

maturity value or face value, or the action of buying financial paper at less than par value before maturity.

(b) In foreign exchange terms, the margin by which the forward exchange rate falls below spot.

(c) In commodity terms, the difference between prices quoted for nearer positions and those more distant.

(d) Lowering of the price allowed for delivery of stocks of a commodity below contract grade against a futures contract.

(e) At below the official rate.

DISCOUNT BOND
Bond selling below par almost always in the secondary market.

DISCOUNT HOUSE
London financial institution dealing in the domestic money market, treasury bills and bills of exchange. There are 12 such houses which have a special relationship with the Bank of England.

DISCOUNT MARKET
UK domestic money market.

DISCOUNT RATE
Interest rate at which a central bank will discount government paper or lend money against government paper collateral. Specifically in the US the rate at which the Federal Reserve will lend short term funds to depository institutions.

DISCOUNT SECURITIES
Money market instruments issued at a discount and redeemed at maturity for the full face value, e.g. Treasury Bills.

DISCOUNT WINDOW
In the US a lending facility provided by the Federal Reserve to eligible depository institutions.

DISCOUNTED CASH FLOW
Accounting techniques for establishing the relative worth

of a future investment project by discounting the expected cash flows from the project against its net present value.

DISCRETIONARY ACCOUNT

Account for which the broker or bank has a discretionary power of attorney, either completely or within set limits, from the holder to manage on his behalf. In the case of a bank, this will involve discretionary funds.

DISEQUILIBRIUM

Imbalance of national or world payments. Under the Bretton Woods system countries were theoretically obliged to adjust their exchange rate or economies when their payments balances moved into fundamental disequilibrium.

DISINTERMEDIATION

Placing of funds directly in securities by investors in a switch away from banks or other financial intermediaries which then place the funds in the credit market.

DISPOSABLE INCOME

Earnings after tax or take home income. Broader than discretionary income, which is net of fixed personal spending commitments as well as tax.

DISTANT DELIVERY OR DISTANTS

See DEFERRED DELIVERIES.

DISTILLATES

Products resulting from condensation during distillation in a refinery, i.e. gaseous fuels, gas and kerosene oils.

DISTILLATION

Refining process which separates or purifies liquids by successive vaporisation and condensation.

DISTRIBUTED PROFITS

Profits distributed to shareholders via dividend payments.

Di

DISTRIBUTION
(a) Distribution of profits as with dividends.
(b) Sale of a large block of stock to a large group of investors in the US.
(c) US Department of Agriculture term for the different potential uses of the available quantities of agricultural commodities.

DIVIDEND
Cash or stock payment to shareholders, variable in the case of ordinary or common shares, fixed in the case of preferred shares. Even if a company is doing badly it may make a payment of past earnings. In the US the payment cannot be greater than the retained earnings account.

DIVIDEND COVER
Number of times a company's dividend is covered by earnings.

DIVIDEND YIELD
Current dividend as a percentage of a share's market price.

DOCKAGE
Waste and foreign material found in grains and oilseeds when grading takes place.

DOCUMENTARY CREDIT
Used in financing foreign trade. It may be confirmed or unconfirmed, revocable or irrevocable. It provides an exporter with immediate payment, while giving an importer credit.

DOLLAR COST AVERAGING
See AVERAGING.

DOUBLE CALL
Sinking fund arrangement giving borrowers an obligation to redeem a fixed number of bonds annually, possibly double the amount due for redemption in that year.

DOUBLE OPTION
Commodity term for the option to buy or sell.

DOUBLE TAXATION
Application of two separate taxes or tax systems to a source of income or capital.

DOW (THE)
Dow Jones industrial average of 30 New York Stock Exchange blue chip stocks.

DOWN TIME
Period when no drilling is possible reflecting poor weather conditions, or technical reasons. Oil term.

DRAUGHT
The distance between the keel of a ship and the water surface. A safe draught allows the vessel to negotiate shallow water and prevents it becoming unstable.

DRAWDOWN
Drawing down funds made available from financial institutions. It can include credits from the International Monetary Fund, Eurocredits from banks or a corporate utilisation of a credit granted by a domestic bank.

DRAWER
Signatory of a bill of exchange requiring the person to whom it is addressed to pay the sum stated on the bill.

DRAWING
Drawing the number of securities (bonds) to be redeemed by lot.

DRILL BIT
Head of a drilling tool which cuts through rock.

DRILL COLLARS
Heavy steel tubing located immediately above the drill bit

to maintain pressure on the bit and keep the drill string in tension.

DRILL SHIP

Vessel with a derrick for drilling in waters which are too deep for a jack-up or semi-submersible rig.

DRILL STEM TEST (DST)

Test of the formation fluids in a possible oil or gas bearing stratum by letting them flow to the surface through the drill string under carefully controlled conditions.

DRILL STRING

Steel piping in approximately 10 metre lengths connecting the bit to the drilling rig. As it rotates, it drills the hole and permits the lubricating mud to circulate. Sometimes called the drill pipe.

DRILLING MUD

Mix of clays, water and chemicals pumped down the drill string to lubricate the system, while carrying away rock cuttings, maintaining pressure at the bit end.

DRILLING PLATFORM

Platform for drilling offshore exploration and development wells but without the processing facilities found on a production platform.

DRILLING RIG

All the equipment needed for drilling a well.

DROPLOCK LOAN

Medium term floating rate facility that automatically becomes a fixed rate bond if interest rates fall to a pre-determined level. For example, a loan with interest of $\frac{3}{4}$ per cent over London interbank offered rates, Libor, could become a fixed rate bond with $13\frac{1}{2}$ per cent interest if, say, yields on government bonds fell below $12\frac{3}{4}$ per cent.

DRY HOLE
Non-productive well, i.e. no gas or oil in commercial quantities.

DRY NATURAL GAS
Natural gas with few associated liquids.

DUAL LISTING
Security which is listed on more than one stock exchange.

DUAL PRICING
Identical product sold at different prices in different markets.

DUE BILL
In the US an instrument evidencing the obligation of a seller to deliver securities to the purchaser. A bill of exchange falling due for payment. Also due date.

DUMPING
Selling goods in a market at low cost, or possibly below cost. It normally involves large quantities of goods sold to export markets.

DUNNAGE
Material used to prevent cargo from coming into contact with the ship's metal structure or other cargo, and thereby suffering damage such as sweating, breakage or chaffing. Materials used include boards, matting and burlap.

DUOPOLY
Market in which there are two dominant sellers of a particular item or service.

DURUM WHEAT
Hard wheat used in making pasta.

DUTCH AUCTION
Auction where the lowest price needed to sell the entire offering is the price at which all the goods being offered for sale are sold.

Dw

DWCC
Deadweight cargo capacity. Shipping term.

DWT
Deadweight tons. Shipping term

DYNAMIC POSITIONING
When a vessel or drill ship is kept on position by computer-controlled propellers rather than by anchors.

EAGGF
See EUROPEAN AGRICULTURAL GUIDANCE AND GUARANTEE FUND.

EAGLE
Ten dollar face value US gold coin.

EARNING ASSETS
Assets which earn income for a bank, corporation.

EARNING POWER
Company's ability to earn sufficient profit to cover its own needs and those of its shareholders.

EARNINGS YIELD
Hypothetical rate of return which an investor would obtain from 100 shares if all the company's latest annual profits were distributed, divided by the current price for 100 shares.

EASE
Slow and/or minor decline in market prices.

EASY MONEY
Lavish availability of credit and money associated with a relaxed monetary policy. Normally, but not always, accompanied by moderate or low interest rates.

Ef

EC
> See EUROPEAN COMMUNITIES.

ECONOMETRICS
> Use of statistical and mathematical methods to verify and develop economic theories. It also covers the development of plans and implementation of policies based on econometric findings.

ECONOMIC AND SOCIAL COMMITTEE
> Advisory body appointed by the EC Council of Ministers representing employers, employees and other interest groups such as consumers.

ECSA
> East Coast South America. Shipping term.

ECU
> See EUROPEAN CURRENCY UNIT

EDGE ACT
> US 1919 act allowing US banks to form subsidiaries to carry out international banking business in the US. Such subsidiaries can operate outside the state in which the parent bank is based.

EDR
> See DEPOSITARY RECEIPT.

EFFECTIVE EXCHANGE RATE
> Composite rate, normally presented as an index intended to reflect the overall performance of a currency against its main trading partners, on a trade weighted basis.

EFFECTIVE THRESHOLD PRICE
> Actual minimum price for cereal imports into the EC from non-member states. It is not the same as the published EC threshold price.

EFFECTIVE YIELD
> Actual rate of return obtained by an investor who acquires and then sells a security.

Ef

EFFICIENT PORTFOLIO
Portfolio providing a maximum expected return for a given risk, or minimum risk for a given return.

EFTA
European Free Trade Association which groups Austria, Iceland, Norway, Portugal, Sweden and Switzerland, while Finland is an associate member. It is linked with the EC through a customs union.

EFTS
Electronic Funds Transfer Systems which switch funds electronically thus avoiding the use of paper.

EITHER OR FACILITY
Arrangement allowing a US concern to borrow Eurodollars from a foreign branch or dollars from the bank's head office.

ELASTICITY
Relative response of one variable to a small percentage change in another, e.g. the degree of change in demand for manufactured exports in response to an exchange rate adjustment; or the change in demand in response to a price change, with more elastic commodities being those least affected by price fluctuation.

ELIGIBLE BANKERS ACCEPTANCE
In the US a bankers acceptance may be 'eligible' if it can be sold by the accepting bank without creating a reserve requirement, or if the Federal Reserve will accept it as collateral at the discount window.

ELIGIBLE BILLS/PAPER
Bills or paper which are eligible for rediscount at the Bank of England.

ELIGIBLE LIABILITIES
Liabilities included in establishing UK banks' reserve asset ratios.

EMBARGO

Prohibition (often official) on the movement by land, sea or air of certain goods, or a ban on trade in general between two countries or a group of countries.

EMS

European Monetary System. Formally introduced in March 1979. Members are West Germany, France, the Netherlands, Belgium, Luxembourg, Italy, Denmark and Ireland. Under EMS rules, no member's currency can move by more than 2.25 per cent against any other member currency. A present exception is Italy, whose currency can move by up to six per cent.

EMU

(a) European Economic and Monetary Union. A long term aim for the Common Market.
(b) European Monetary Unit, a currency basket used in some commercial bond issues.

ENDORSEMENT

Writing of a signature on the back of a bill or document. For a bill of exchange or security certificate such a signature transfers ownership of the bill or security.

ENTREPOT

Literally a warehouse. Also a major international trading centre to which goods are shipped for re-export elsewhere, i.e. entrepot trade.

ENTREPRENEUR

Someone who puts up the funds for an enterprise, and thus undertakes the risk.

ENTRY PRICE

Price for certain imported farm products at EC frontiers.

EQUALISATION TAX

A duty under the EC Common Agricultural Policy aimed

Eq

at equalising the import price of non-EC products with the price for similar goods produced within the Common Market.

EQUILIBRIUM

Balance or near balance in a country's external payments position, or in the payments balances of a group of major IMF nations.

EQUIPMENT TRUST CERTIFICATE

Security or bond issued (mainly in the US) to pay for new equipment, and secured on the equipment. Ownership is held by a trustee until the debt is repaid. Used to purchase aircraft, railway equipment, etc.

EQUITY

(a) Common stock, or net worth, of a company;
(b) In US commodities markets the remaining value of a futures trading account if it is disposed of at current market prices.

EQUIVALENT BOND YIELD

A US measure to assess the true annual yield on a short term non-interest bearing security bought on a discount basis. It is used to compare Treasury Bill nominal returns with yields on securities.

ESCALATOR CLAUSE

(a) Clause in a wage contract giving automatic pay increases when the cost of living rises beyond agreed thresholds.
(b) Clause in a contract, typically a capital project, allowing a price increase payable to the contractor to help offset cost inflation.

ESCROW

Agreement or deed involving three parties. The third party is responsible for custody of the deed, which does not take legal effect until the grantee (the person obtaining a benefit from the performance of the deed) fulfils certain conditions.

ETHANE

Colourless, odourless gas, sometimes extracted from natural gas as feedstock for the chemical industry.

EUA

See UNIT OF ACCOUNT.

EURCO

European Composite (currency) Unit. Private sector unit of account based on EC currencies. First used in 1973, it also included sterling.

EUROBOND

International straight or convertible bond issued by state or corporate entities, denominated in a Eurocurrency, and issued outside the currency's domicile. Normally sold on several international markets by groups or syndicates of banks or brokers in units equivalent to one thousand US dollars.

EUROCLEAR

Computerised clearing system for Eurobonds operated and managed under contract by the Brussels *branch* of Morgan *Guaranty* Trust Co of New York.

EUROCREDIT

Medium term international credits in a Eurocurrency usually provided by a syndicate of banks. Such credits are normally for a fixed term with an agreed margin, and base rate, e.g. Libor, (the London interbank offered rate) for six month deposits in the Eurocurrency being used.

EUROCURRENCY

Bank deposit made and held outside the country of the currency's domestic origin, e.g. Euromarks, Euro French francs, Euro Swiss francs, Eurosterling, Euroguilder, Euroyen etc.

EURODOLLAR

Most extensively used Eurocurrency. A dollar deposit outside the US.

Eu

EUROMARKET
Overall term for international capital markets dealing in Eurobonds, Eurocredits, etc.

EUROPEAN AGRICULTURAL GUIDANCE AND GUARANTEE FUND (EAGGF)
Also known by its French abbreviation FEOGA. The fund is used to finance the EC's Common Agricultural Policy.

EUROPEAN CURRENCY UNIT (ECU)
Currency basket at the centre of the EMS. A notional currency made up from EMS member states differing shares of EC output. See EMS.

EUROPEAN DEPOSITARY RECEIPT
See AMERICAN DEPOSITARY RECEIPT and DEPOSITARY RECEIPT.

EUROPEAN COMMUNITIES (EC)
European Common Market, made up of 10 member states. Belgium, France, Italy, Luxembourg, the Netherlands and West Germany. Established in 1957 under the Treaty of Rome. Denmark, Ireland and the UK joined in 1973 followed by Greece in 1981. Portugal and Spain are now seeking full membership.

EUROPEAN FREE TRADE ASSOCIATION
See EFTA.

EUROPEAN INVESTMENT BANK
Long term financing body of the EC, which also provides 'soft' loans to developing countries associated with the community. See SOFT LOAN.

EUROPEAN MONETARY CO-OPERATION FUND
Also known by French abbreviation FECOM. Finances and settles claims by EC central banks on each other resulting from intervention under the European Monetary System.

EUROPEAN MONETARY SYSTEM
See EMS.

EUROPEAN PARLIAMENT
Directly elected assembly of representatives from the member states of the EC. It acts in a consultative and deliberative role and makes recommendations to the EC Council. It is the only body which can dismiss the EC Commission.

EUROSYNDICATED LOANS
Large bank credits, usually with maturities of three to ten years granted by international bank syndicates put together on an ad hoc basis. Lenders are almost exclusively banks and finance companies, thus these credits are not placed with private investors. Interest rates are calculated by adding a margin to interbank offered rates and usually adjusted every three or six months. Funds for the loans are drawn from the Euromarket.

EVEN LOT
Commodity trading unit governed by official exchange price quotations.

EVENING UP
Buying and selling to offset an existing market position.

EVERGREEN CREDIT
Revolving credit with no fixed maturity date, which a bank has the option once annually to convert into a term loan.

EX ALL
Excluding all supplementary advantages attaching to a share. Opposite is cum all.

EX CAP
Ex capitalisation, excluding the rights of scrip or capitalisation issues attaching to a share. Opposite is cum cap.

EX COUPON
Without taking into account the coupon, i.e. if a bond is sold

ex coupon, the seller will not receive the payment due on the coupon. Opposite is cum coupon.

EX DIV

Ex dividend, excluding the right to the current dividend on a share. Opposite is cum dividend.

EX FACTORY/MILL/WAREHOUSE

Delivery term based on the price quoted, i.e. the buyer will pick up the goods at the factory.

EX PIT TRANSACTIONS

Trades executed outside the exchange trading ring or pit. Mainly used for fixing prices when cash commodities are being bought.

EX QUAY

Goods available at the quayside. Shipping term.

EX RIGHTS

Excluding the rights to an issue of shares for cash made by a company to its existing shareholder. Opposite is cum rights.

EX SHIP

Price quoted for goods on arrival at a port. It does not include costs of unloading and delivery to the premises of the buyer.

EX STORE

Term relating to the sale of commodities currently held in a warehouse or other storage facility.

EXCESS LIQUIDITY

Banks having liquidity, cash or cash instruments, over and above their normal requirements.

EXCESS RESERVES

US bank-held reserves with the Federal Reserve in excess of requirements. It is the difference between total reserves eligible to meet reserve requirements and required reserves that must be held.

EXCHANGE ACQUISITION

Method of filling an order to purchase a large block of stock on the floor of the New York Stock Exchange, by seeking sell orders and then crossing them with the buy order.

EXCHANGE CERTIFIED STOCKS

See CERTIFICATED STOCKS.

EXCHANGE CONTROLS

Regulations designed to restrict or prevent certain foreign currency transactions mainly by a country's nationals. Also likely to cover movement of precious metals, especially gold and silver. Controls are used to maintain and protect a country's financial position and the value of its currency.

EXCHANGE DISTRIBUTION

Method of filling an order to sell a large block of stock on the floor of the New York Stock Exchange, by seeking buy orders and crossing them with the sell order.

EXCHANGE EQUALISATION ACCOUNT

Account controlled by the UK Treasury and managed by the Bank of England. Its assets include the country's gold and foreign exchange reserves and the objective is to manage the exchange in line with government policy. Many countries operate similar accounts. In the US and France they are known as Exchange Stabilisation Funds.

EXCHANGE FOR PHYSICAL

Also called exchange for cash. A situation where the buyer of a cash commodity transfers to the seller an equivalent amount of long futures contracts, or receives from him a corresponding amount of short futures at an agreed price.

EXCHANGE RATE

Rate at which a currency is exchanged for another currency, gold or Special Drawing Rights. See PARITY.

Ex

EXECUTION BY OUTCRY
Commodity exchange orders transacted by verbal offer and acceptance in the trading ring or pit.

EXEMPT SECURITIES
Securities in the US which are exempt from certain Securities and Exchange Commission registration and margin requirements. These include government, agency and municipal securities as well as commercial paper and private placements. See SECURITIES AND EXCHANGE COMMISSION.

EXERCISE NOTICE
When the holder of an option gives formal notice of intent to exercise his right to buy the underlying stock at the previously fixed price.

EXOTIC CURRENCIES
Currencies which are infrequently dealt, and in which there is no international market of any size.

EXPIRY NOTICE
Last day for exercising an option. See DECLARATION DATE.

EXPORT HOUSES
Trading houses specialising in selling virtually all categories of goods throughout the world. They can handle all aspects of international trade, including finance.

EXPORT QUOTA
(a) Quota set under an international commodity agreement, whereby exporting countries of a particular commodity accept limits on their exports.
(b) Bilateral or multilateral agreement between countries governing exports of industrial or other goods.

EXPORT REFUNDS
Refunds (or restitutions) made under the EC's Common Agricultural Policy on exports of grain. The refunds are

intended to help exports by offsetting the difference between the internal EC price and lower world prices.

EXPOSURE
(a) When a bank provides funds to a country or corporation, it becomes exposed to the borrower. Most banks have internal rules designed to prevent involvement in over exposure to any single borrower.
(b) On foreign exchange markets, exposure can arise through the existence of an uncovered position, whether overall or for a single currency. The extent of exposure can reflect the different maturity periods for the currencies being used.

EXTENDABLE MATURITY
Security where the investor has the option at certain specified dates to extend the maturity.

EXTENDED FUND FACILITY (EFF)
Assistance provided to IMF member countries with economies suffering from serious balance of payment difficulties due to structural imbalances in production, trade and prices or economies characterised by slow growth and an inherently weak balance of payments position. Drawings can be made over a period of three years under conditions similar to IMF standby drawings.

EXTERNAL ACCOUNTS
Accounts in a national currency maintained for use by non-residents.

EXTRACTION INDUSTRY
Industry involved in extracting raw materials from the land, sea or air.

EXTRACTION RATE
Proportion by weight of a processed product to its raw material.

Fa

FAC

Fast as can. A vessel will load or discharge as fast as she can take on board or unload. This implies an obligation upon the part of the charterer to supply the cargo as fast as the ship requires it. The term should not be read as obligation to take cargo at a rate which is in excess of the customary daily discharging rate of the port.

FACE VALUE

Apparent worth. The nominal value which appears on the face of a document recording an entitlement, generally a certificate or bond. For indebtedness, the amount to be repaid at maturity.

FACILITY FEE

Charge paid by borrowers to banks for the extension of a credit facility.

FACTOR

Agent who transacts business for another on a commission basis.

FACTORING

Service which enables a company to collect money on credit sales, the factor purchasing the company's invoiced debts for cash but at a discount, and then seeking repayment from the original purchaser of the company's goods or services.

FAE

Free Alongside Elevator. Shipping term.

FANNIE MAE

See FEDERAL NATIONAL MORTGAGE ASSOCIA-TION.

FAO

See FOOD AND AGRICULTURAL ORGANISATION.

FAQ

Fair Average Quality. Used in the sale of agricultural

commodities, i.e. average grade based on samples rather than on a specific grade.

FARM OUT
Arranging for part of a production process, an ancillary service, or the drilling of an oil well to be performed by an independent specialist or group of companies.

FAS
(a) In the US, to the Financial Accounting Standards which govern accounting rules.
(b) In shipping, free alongside. A charterer's responsibility for delivering goods on quay within reach of ship's cranes etc.

FATS AND OILS
Key products in international commodity and agricultural trade. They comprise animal fats and vegetable oils.

FCIA
See FOREIGN CREDIT INSURANCE ASSOCIATION.

FCM
See FUTURES COMMISSION MERCHANT.

FD
Free discharge. The cost of unloading a vessel is paid by the charterer. Shipping term.

FECOM
See EUROPEAN MONETARY CO-OPERATION FUND.

FED
See FEDERAL RESERVE SYSTEM.

FED FUNDS
See FEDERAL FUNDS.

Fe

FEDERAL CREDIT AGENCIES
US federal government sponsored agencies providing credit to different groups of institutions and persons. Many are privately owned.

FEDERAL DEPOSIT INSURANCE CORP (FDIC)
Established in US in 1933 to insure accounts at commercial and mutual savings banks and thus protect depositors. All Federal Reserve members are required to be members. It has federal supervisory authority over insured state banks not members of the Federal Reserve.

FEDERAL FINANCING BANK
Obtains funds from the US Treasury for lending to federal credit agencies.

FEDERAL FUNDS
Reserve balances that US depository institutions lend each other, usually on an overnight basis. Federal Funds also include some other kinds of borrowings by depository institutions from each other and federal agencies.

FEDERAL HOME LOAN BANKS (FHLB)
Comprise 12 US banks and the FHLB board. They oversee the operations of all federal savings and loans associations and federally insured state chartered Savings and Loans as well as providing finance.

FEDERAL NATIONAL MORTGAGE ASSOCIATION (FNMA)
Or Fannie Mae. Established and supervised by the US federal government FNMA is a privately owned entity. Its main role is to maintain a secondary market in conventional and government-underwritten mortgages.

FEDERAL OPEN MARKET COMMITTEE (FOMC)
This 12 member policy committee of the US Federal Reserve

system meets periodically to set Federal Reserve guidelines, followed by the Federal Reserve Bank of New York's open market desk in buying and selling government securities in the open market as a means of influencing the volume and cost of bank credit and money. The FOMC also establishes policy relating to operations in the foreign exchange markets.

FEDERAL RESERVE SYSTEM

Known as the Fed, this is the central banking system of the United States comprising 12 Federal Reserve Banks controlling 12 districts under the Federal Reserve Board in Washington. Membership of the Fed is obligatory for banks chartered by the US Comptroller of Currency and voluntary for banks chartered with state charters. All member banks subscribe to its capital and around 70 per cent of US bank deposits are held by member banks. About 37 per cent of all banks are members. The 12 Fed banks are based in Boston, New York, Philadelphia, Cleveland, Richmond, Atlanta, Chicago, St Louis, Dallas, Minneapolis, Kansas City and San Francisco.

FEDWIRE

The US Federal Reserve's electronic communications system linking Federal Reserve Offices, the Board, depository institions, the Treasury and other government agencies. Used for transferring the reserve account balances of depository institutions and government securities.

FEED CONCENTRATES

Term covering corn (maize), sorghum, barley, oats, wheat, rye, oilseed meal, used in the production of animal feeds.

FEED GRAINS

Also coarse grains. Corn, sorghum, barley, and oats as well as feed wheat, feed rye.

FEED RATIOS

Relationship between the cost of feeding animals and their market price expressed as a ratio.

Fe

FEEDSTOCK

Provision of crude oil, natural gas liquids or natural gas to a refinery or petrochemical plant, or the supply of an intermediate petrochemical.

FEFAC

Federation Européenne des Fabricants d'Aliments Composés pour Animaux. The Brussels-based European Federation of Manufacturers of Animal Feed Compounds.

FHEX

Fridays and holidays excluded. Refers to unloading and loading which will not be carried out during official holidays nor on Fridays in Islamic countries. Shipping term.

FIDUCIARY ISSUE

Issue of notes not backed by precious metals, i.e. issued in faith.

FIFO

First in, first out. A principle of accounting by which the valuation of a company's stocks is based on the assumption that goods are used in the order of purchase; thus, those bought earlier (first) are used earlier (first). Opposite to LIFO, last in, first out.

FINAL DIVIDEND

Dividend paid out by a company at the end of its financial year. See Dividend.

FINANCIAL YEAR

Year used for accounting purposes. It may be the same as the calendar year or cover a different period, e.g. April to March. Normally but not always for 12 months. Also called Fiscal Year.

FINE RATE

Low rate of interest on a loan. Lowest acceptable rates with narrow bid and offer rates.

Fi

FINE TUNING

Flexible fiscal and monetary policy action designed to achieve precise short term patterns of economic performance.

FINENESS

Quality or purity of precious metals.

FIO

Free in and out. The cost of loading and unloading is borne by the shipowner or shipper and not the party chartering the ship.

FIRM

(a) Advancing market.
(b) Buy or sell order which can be carried out without further confirmation during a fixed period.
(c) On the foreign exchange market, a 'firm' quote means a dealer is willing to trade at the rate thus quoted.

FIRMER

Market which is rising, particularly after some hesitancy.

FIRST LINE RESERVES

Currency component of a central bank's monetary reserves, a non-US term.

FIRST NOTICE DAY

First day on which sellers of commodities can inform purchasers, through the clearing house, of their intent to deliver actual commodities against futures contracts.

FISCAL AGENT

In the Eurobond market a bank which is appointed agent for an issue, including acting as principal paying agent.

FISCAL DRAG

Inhibiting effect on private economic activity of the automatic growth in government revenue taken from its income and cash resources.

Fi

FISCAL YEAR
See FINANCIAL YEAR.

FISHMEAL
Fish processed into meal and used for livestock and poultry feed after extracting fish oil.

FIX
(a) On some foreign exchange markets or bourses a daily meeting (fixing) at which rates for different currencies are officially fixed by adjusting the buying and selling level to reflect market conditions. Participants include commercial banks and directly or indirectly the central bank. The latter may intervene to maintain a rate at a specific level.

(b) On the gold market the twice daily meeting at 1030 and 1500 of the five London bullion houses at which they fix the gold price by matching bids and offers.

(c) For floating rate securities or loans, a meeting shortly before the start of each new interest period to fix the interest rate level.

FIXATION
Point at which the buyer or seller in a call purchase or sale on a futures market determines the price, i.e. the purchaser in a sale, the seller in a purchase.

FIXED ASSETS
Land, buildings, plant, equipment, and other assets acquired for carrying on the business of a company with a life exceeding one year. Normally expressed in accounts at cost, less accumulated depreciation.

FIXED CAPITAL
Similar to Fixed Assets except purchased out of paid up capital.

FIXED CHARGES
Operational or business expenses which are fixed and have no set relation to varying output levels.

FIXED DATES
> Fixed or standard periods for trading Eurodeposits, which range from one month to a year.

FIXED DEPOSIT
> Deposit repayable on a set future date with a fixed interest for the whole period.

FIXED EXCHANGE RATE
> Exchange value with fixed parities, or central rate relationships with SDRs, gold, the US dollar or other currencies. See SPECIAL DRAWING RIGHTS (SDRs.)

FIXED RATE LOAN
> Loan for a fixed period of time with a fixed interest rate for the life of the loan.

FIXING
> See FIX.

FLARING
> Burning off gas resulting from oil extraction which cannot be stored, reinjected or shipped ashore.

FLASH POINT
> Lowest temperature at which vapour from oil will ignite when briefly exposed to a source of ignition.

FLAT INCOME BOND
> A bond traded in the US where the price includes consideration for all unpaid accruals of interest.

FLAT YIELD
> See CURRENT YIELD.

FLEET POLICY
> Marine insurance policy covering vessels operated by a single ownership or management. Shipping Term.

Fl

FLEXIBLE TARIFF
In the US a tariff designed to even out differences between the cost of imported and domestically produced goods.

FLOAT
(a) Condition under which a currency is allowed to fluctuate outside internationally prescribed limits without discretionary intervention, i.e. free float. See DIRTY FLOAT.

(c) To launch an issue, company or business.

(b) In the US term to describe the timelag which often occurs in the Federal Reserve's cheque collection process. The Federal Reserve credits the reserve accounts of depository institutions within two business days of the cheques being deposited, but more time may be needed to process some cheques and receive funds in payment. Thus some institutions may receive credit before the Federal Reserve has obtained payment from others.

FLOATING CHARGE
Charge or assignment on a company's total assets as collateral for a loan.

FLOATING DEBT
Short term debt, specifically short term government debt. Also called unfunded debt.

FLOATING PRIME RATE
Prime rate movements under various automatic formulae. See PRIME RATE.

FLOATING RATE BOND
Bond with a variable interest rate.

FLOATING RATE CD
Certificate of deposit with a variable interest rate, normally linked to the London interbank money market rate. See CERTIFICATE OF DEPOSIT.

FLOATING RATE NOTE
Debt security with a maturity of five to seven years. The interest rate is adjusted to money market conditions usually every six months (some are three months) with a minimum rate normally guaranteed.

FLOATING SUPPLY
Quantity of securities or commodities readily available for immediate sale or purchase in stock or commodity market.

FLOOR
Trading floor in a stock exchange or commodity market.

FLOOR BROKER
Exchange member who executes orders for others on the floor of the exchange and is paid commission.

FLOOR PRICE
Minimum price which normally cannot be further reduced due to political, economic or trade considerations.

FLOOR TRADER
Exchange member who usually effects orders on his own account, or one in which he has an interest, on the trading floor.

FLOW OF FUNDS ANALYSIS
Analysis of the origin and use of funds in the different sectors of the economy.

FLOWER BONDS
Low coupon US Treasury bonds acceptable at par in payment of federal estates tax when a person dies.

FLUSH TWEENDECKER
Tweendecker whose hatches are level with the flooring so that vehicles can move over the floor freely. Shipping term. See TWEENDECKER.

Fo

FOB (FREE ON BOARD)
(a) Cost of loading a ship is borne by the charterer. FOB and trimmed is used in the coal shipment trade to indicate that the coal must also be properly stowed.

(b) Applied to imports in balance of payments accounts to mean valuation of goods at point of embarkation. This makes imports more directly comparable to exports. See CIF.

FOOD & AGRICULTURAL ORGANISATION (FAO)
A United Nations organisation established to improve world agriculture, fishing and forestry. Based in Rome it also provides technical assistance, food aid and issues forecasts and statistics on the world agricultural outlook.

FOOD BALANCE
Overall availability of food supplies compared with the population to be fed.

FORCE MAJEURE
Occurrence outside the control of parties to a contract. A force majeure clause exempts the parties from their obligations under the contract if such an occurrence, e.g. an earthquake or typhoon, takes place.

FOREIGN BOND ISSUE
Bond issue for a foreign borrower/guarantor underwritten by a bank or bank syndicate in one particular country, denominated in the currency of that country, placed and traded mainly within that country.

FOREIGN CREDIT INSURANCE ASSOCIATION (FCIA)
US corporation owned by insurance companies providing export credit insurance.

FOREIGN EXCHANGE
Claims to foreign currency payable abroad, including bank

deposits, bills, cheques. Foreign exchange rates refer to the number of units of one currency needed to buy another.

FORMA
Fonds d'Organisation et Regularisation des Marchés Agricoles. French governmental organisation aimed at stabilising farm prices. It also acts as the intervention organisation in France for a number of products governed by EC agricultural policy rules.

FORTIFIED FOODS
Foods to which vitamins, minerals, protein etc. have been added to improve their nutritional qualities.

FORWARD BOOK
Foreign exchange term for the total of net forward positions in various currencies, reflecting either current trading or a bank's views on a specific currency.

FORWARD CONTRACT
Contract for settlement of a foreign exchange transaction at any date later than spot.

FORWARD CONTRACTING
Cash transaction under which the buyer and seller agree on the delivery of a specified quality and quantity of a commodity or other goods at a specified future date. The price may be fixed beforehand or at delivery.

FORWARD COVER
Arrangement by a purchaser or seller of foreign exchange to cover himself against unforeseen exchange rate movements through a forward foreign exchange contract. See COVER.

FORWARD EXCHANGE RATE
Rate at which a currency can be purchased or sold for delivery in the future.

Fo

FORWARD FORWARD
Simultaneous purchase and sale of one currency for different maturity dates in the forward market by means of:
(a) Contract providing for the future delivery of a deposit maturing on a further forward date.
(b) Contract providing for the future delivery at a fixed price of a deposit maturing on a further forward date, i.e. creating a forward deposit.

FORWARD INTERVENTION
Intervention by a central bank in forward markets aimed at influencing a currency's spot rate. It can also involve a central bank acting to influence forward interest rates in its currency.

FORWARD MARGIN
Discount or premium between the spot and forward rates for a currency.

FORWARD MARKET
Market in foreign exchange for future delivery or in physical commodities for later shipment. In the US it can also mean trading outside a commodity exchange for delivery at a future date.

FORWARD MATURITIES
Days beyond spot for which forward deals can be completed.

FORWARD MONTHS
Months in which futures contracts for forward delivery are traded.

FORWARD PURCHASE
Purchase for delivery of a commodity at a later date. Opposite is forward sale.

FORWARD SHIPMENT
Agreement for the shipment of cash commodities at a set future date.

FOW

First open water. Usually refers to start of navigation after the winter freeze, especially in the Great Lakes and St Lawrence seaway. Shipping term.

FOUL BILL OF LADING

See DIRTY BILL OF LADING.

FR

Full range of ports. Shipping term.

FRACTIONS

Liquid hydrocarbons with a given boiling range, produced during the fractional distillation process.

FRACTIONAL DISTILLATION

Separation of crude oil or one of its components into liquids of different boiling ranges (fractions) by distillation; the basic process occurring in an oil refinery.

FRACTIONATING COLUMN

Tall tower in which fractional distillation takes place and which produces different distillates.

FRANC ZONE

Currency zone grouping most former French West African colonies and French dependencies in the Pacific co-ordinated and assisted by the Banque de France. It uses the CFA and CFP francs.

FREE ALONGSIDE SHIP

See FAS.

FREE (AND OPEN) MARKET

Supply and demand fixing market price levels, without the influence of any outside factors.

Fr

FREE OF DELIVERY
Payment for securities without necessarily involving immediate delivery.

FREE ON BOARD
See FOB. Shipping term.

FREE ON RAIL (FOR)
Price of goods which includes the cost of moving them to a railhead for shipment. Free on truck (FOT) is a similar term for road transport.

FREE PORT
Coastal or inland port where goods are not required to pay duties or taxes.

FREE RESERVES
Margin by which excess reserves exceed borrowings at Federal Reserve banks.

FREE SUPPLY
Commodity stocks available for sale, as opposed to government-owned or controlled stocks.

FREEBOARD
Distance between the waterline and a ship's main deck.

FREEDOM TYPE VESSEL
See LIBERTY TYPE VESSEL.

FREIGHT
(a) Sum or fee paid for chartering a ship, or carrying its cargo.
(b) Cargo usually transported by land, sea or air.

FRONT END FEES
Fees paid when a loan is arranged, such as management fees.

FRONT END FINANCE

Finance provided during the early stages of a contract or project in export contracts. It is often used to finance that part of the purchase price not covered by export credits.

FRONT END LOADING

Charges or fees which are greater at the start of a loan or investment contract than in its later stages.

FROZEN ASSETS

Assets, balances or credits temporarily blocked or frozen due to political circumstances, e.g. war, or legal action.

FUNDAMENTAL ANALYSIS

Also called fundamental research. System of analysing the basic underlying factors affecting the outlook for supply and demand for a security or commodity and the resulting price outlook.

FUNDAMENTAL DISEQUILIBRIUM

Generally refers to a basic and serious imbalance in a country's balance of payments, thus providing justification for devaluation or revaluation by a government under IMF rules governing exchange rate management.

FUNDED DEBT

Long term indebtedness of a corporation or a government resulting from the conversion of short term debt. In the UK refers to undated government stock providing an income yield whose principal the government need only repay when it wishes to do so.

FUNDING

Process of converting short term fixed interest debt to long term fixed interest debt.

FUNGIBILITY

Interchangeability. Something fungible can be exchanged for another answering the same description. Thus one five pound note is fungible as it can be changed for another five pound note. On a futures market, contracts for the same commodity and delivery month are fungible as such contracts have to meet standard specifications.

FUTURES

Contracts for the purchase or sale of financial instruments or physical commodities for future delivery on a commodity exchange.

FUTURES COMMISSION MERCHANT

Individual or legal entity registered with the CFTC in the US who solicits business from others for execution on a listed commodity exchange.

FUTURES MARKET

Organised exchange where contracts for the future delivery of various commodities are traded according to established rules and regulations.

FWAD

Fresh water arrival draft. Shipping term.

FX

Foreign exchange.

G-10

See GROUP OF TEN.

GAB

See GENERAL ARRANGEMENTS TO BORROW.

GARAGE

(a) To transfer assets or liabilities elsewhere, either to a different centre or different company normally with the intention of reducing tax liability.
(b) One of the floor sections on the New York Stock Exchange.

GAS OIL

Petroleum distillates from the oil refining process, intermediate between light and lubricating oils and kerosene. Used to produce diesel fuel and for burning in certain central heating systems.

GAS TO OIL RATIO

Number of cubic feet of gas per barrel of oil at atmospheric pressure, or as the volume of gas to volume of oil.

G

GASIFICATION

Manufacture of gaseous fuel from a solid or liquid fuel.

GASOLINE

Light petroleum distillate used in spark ignited petroleum combustion engines. Equivalent to motor spirit or petrol.

GATT

See GENERAL AGREEMENT ON TARIFFS AND TRADE.

GDP

See GROSS DOMESTIC PRODUCT.

GEARED

Vessel which has heavy lifts and/or cranes.

GEARING

Relationship between loan capital, preference capital and ordinary capital. It can be expressed in terms of either nominal value or market capitalisation value. High gearing means that prior charges and/or senior issues are large in relation to the equity or ordinary shares. Low gearing means the reverse.

GEARLESS

Vessel which has little or no means for loading and unloading cargo.

Ge

GEL

Mud able to hold solids in suspension when normal circulation by pumping is interrupted. Oil term.

GEN SAKI MARKET

Market run by Japanese securities houses to sell bonds in the secondary market with a repurchase agreement. Because the supply of non-government bonds is tight, market values tend to rise, permitting the buyer to receive both interest and spread on the price between the purchase and the sale. It competes with bank-run markets, such as those for certificates of deposit and call money.

GENERAL AGREEMENT ON TARIFFS AND TRADE (GATT)

Established in Geneva in 1948 as a legislative and negotiating framework for international trade relations.

GENERAL ARRANGEMENTS TO BORROW (GAB)

Arrangement set up in 1962 involving the members of the Group of Ten and Switzerland under which the countries concerned agreed to provide special credits to the IMF in their own currencies for G-10 member countries. The GAB needs the collective agreement of its members to be activated. The credits are separate from the IMF's normal resources and are only for use by a GAB member facing currency or payments difficulties.

GENERAL AVERAGE LOSS

Marine insurance term for a loss at sea as the result of a deliberate act intended to save the ship as a whole, or at least part of the cargo. Jettisoning burning cargo to save the rest of the ship is such a loss, which is shared between the owners of the cargo and the shipowner.

GENERAL MORTGAGE BOND

US securities term for a bond secured by a blanket mortgage on a corporation's property.

GENERAL OBLIGATION BOND

US tax exempt debt of a state or local government which is secured by the issuer's full faith, credit and taxing powers.

GENERALISED SYSTEM OF PREFERENCES (GSP)

Tariff cuts and quota increases intended to encourage exports from developing countries.

GILT EDGED

Highest quality securities in UK. Normally applies only to government stocks which are gilt edged as there is virtually no default risk attached to them. Sometimes used to include nationalised or municipal securities, which do not strictly fall into the same category.

GILTS

Abbreviation for gilt edged.

GINNIE MAE (GNMA)

See GOVERNMENT NATIONAL MORTGAGE AS-SOCIATION

GIVE UP

Loss in yield from the sale of securities at one yield and the purchase of a similar amount of other securities with a lower yield.

GL

Great Lakes. Shipping term.

GLASS STEAGALL

US law of 1933 prohibiting commercial banks from under-writing or dealing in securities except for general obligation bonds and in selected special purpose municipal revenue bonds and US government debts.

Gn

GNMA
See GOVERNMENT NATIONAL MORTGAGE ASSOCIATION.

GNP
See GROSS NATIONAL PRODUCT.

GO AROUND
Calls by the Federal Reserve, while conducting open market operations, to primary dealers in US government securities. By thus going around it informs whether it wants to purchase or sell securities, do repurchases or reverses and then seeks bids or offers.

GODOWN
Warehouse or storage facility in the Far East.

GOGO FUND
High risk investment fund or unit trust intended to produce a greater than average increase in value by speculation.

GOLD CERTIFICATE
Document certifying the ownership of gold held at an authorised or recognised depository, mainly in the US.

GOLD CLAUSE
Repayment to be linked to the value of gold, or in gold itself.

GOLD EXCHANGE STANDARD
When a national currency cannot be used by residents to purchase gold from their central bank, and when the latter does not hold a large gold element in its reserve. Instead these reserves are held in the currency of a country allowing convertibility of its own currency into gold e.g. the US dollar until 1971. This is known as the gold exchange standard.

Go

GOLD FIX

Routine twice daily fixing at 1030 and 1500 of the free market gold price by the five participating London bullion houses. The fix involves a matching of the bid and offer price.

GOLD FRANC

Different gold francs are still used under various international agreements as a method of calculating assets and liabilities under these agreements e.g. Poincaré franc for shipping. The balance sheet of the Bank for International Settlements BIS is defined in gold francs. The value of these gold francs used by the BIS is now expressed in terms of the SDR since there is no longer an official gold price. See SPECIAL DRAWING RIGHT (SDR.)

GOLD POOL

Agreement of 1961 among the central banks of Britain, Belgium, France, Italy, Netherlands, West Germany, Switzerland and the US intended to stabilise the gold price at close to the then official parity of 35 US dollars an ounce. It broke up in 1968 after France renounced its membership in 1967.

GOLD RESERVES

Gold bullion content of a central bank's monetary reserves.

GOLD SHARES

Shares in gold mining companies, mainly South African and Australian.

GOLD STANDARD

Monetary system in which the gold value of a currency is fixed by law and the authorities, on demand, have to be prepared to exchange gold at a given rate for the currency. It was abandoned by most countries in 1931.

GOLD TRANCHE

First 25 per cent of a member country's quota with the IMF which had to be subscribed in gold though it might be less for

Go

new members with reserve difficulties. The remainder of the quota was in the member's domestic currency. A country could draw automatically, and without condition, on the IMF to the value of its gold tranche.

GOOD DELIVERY
Delivery of securities or commodities in good and due form; a delivery which meets contract conditions.

GOOD TILL CANCELLED (GTC)
Buy or sell order which remains in force until executed, or cancelled, by the customer. Also called Open Order.

GOODWILL
Reputation or intangible value of a business or company. Classified as an asset, it is the purchase value of an acquisition less the book value of its assets. In the US it is amortised over 40 years.

GOVERNMENT BROKER
Stockbroker appointed to act as the government's agent in the British government bond market. This is traditionally the senior partner of the firm of Mullens & Co.

GOVERNMENT NATIONAL MORTGAGE ASSOCIATION (GNMA)
Or Ginnie Mae. Set up in the US in 1968 to take over some of the functions of the Federal National Mortgage Association. Securities issued by the GNMA are backed pools of mortgages. They bear a US government guarantee and are traded in an active secondary market.

GRACE PERIOD
Length of time during which repayments of loan principal are excused. Occurs at the start of the loan period, often in connection with soft loans to developing countries, where the terms and conditions are mild.

GREEN CURRENCY
Notional currency used when implementing Common Agri-

cultural Policy rates, sometimes called Green Rate. The currencies of EC member states are fixed in terms of European units of account. These fixed values are known as green currencies, i.e. artificial exchange rates. Thus the value of a member state's currency in the sphere of agricultural produce is fixed by administrative decision rather than by free market forces.

GREY MARKET
Unofficial market, not subject to official controls.

GROSS DOMESTIC PRODUCT (GDP)
Similar to Gross National Product but omits income from abroad.

GROSS NATIONAL PRODUCT (GNP)
The total value of goods and services produced within a period of time, by an economy, including government and private spending, fixed capital investment, net inventory changes, net exports. Real GNP growth describes the increase in national output after abstracting inflation.

GROSS NATIONAL PRODUCT DEFLATOR
Method to establish the actual growth in the output of goods and services by eliminating growth due to price increases. Normally expressed as a percentage and based on an index figure.

GROSS NATIONAL PRODUCT GAP
Gap between actual real GNP and potential real GNP under full employment conditions. When the gap turns negative, an economy is said to be overheated.

GROSS PRICE
Price before any deduction is made as opposed to net price, e.g. in the US securities market, exclusive of any commission.

Gr

GROSS PROCESSING MARGIN
Difference between the cost of raw materials and the sales revenue from finished products.

GROSS PROFIT
Total profit before deduction of tax and expenses.

GROSS REGISTER TONS (GRT)
Total enclosed capacity in a ship in units of 100 cubic feet, less certain exempted spaces.

GROSS SPREAD
Difference between the price received by an issuer for its securities and the price paid by investors for the same securities. The spread equals the selling concession, together with the management and underwriting fees.

GROSS TERMS
Cost of loading and unloading a ship is borne by the ship-owner.

GROSS YIELD
Pretax return on a security.

GROSS YIELD TO REDEMPTION
Yield in the UK on a security if held to redemption, including an estimated annual capital gain, but excluding income or capital gains tax.

GROUP OF TEN (G-10)
Main industrialised countries within the framework of the IMF. Members are Britain, Belgium, Canada, France, Italy, Japan, Netherlands, Sweden, the US and West Germany. Switzerland, which is not an IMF member, is associated with most G-10 meetings. See also GAB.

GROUP OF 77
Comprises 122 countries and was established to help promote

the views of developing countries on international trade and development in UNCTAD. Originally established with 77 countries. See UNCTAD.

GROWTH PROSPECTS

Prospects a company may have of further fast high profit development, and whose shares may therefore be expected to increase in value.

GROWTH STOCKS

Shares of a publicly owned company with growth prospects.

GROWTHS

Type of coffee, cocoa, cotton etc. according to area or country in which it is produced.

GRT

See GROSS REGISTER TONS.

GSP

See GENERALISED SYSTEM OF PREFERENCES.

GTC

See GOOD TILL CANCELLED.

GUARANTEED BOND

US market term for a bond where the interest and principal or both are guaranteed by a person or corporation other than the issuer.

GUARANTEED STOCK

Normally refers to preferred stock in the US whose dividend is guaranteed.

GUIDE PRICE

One of the pricing systems used with the EC's Common Agricultural Policy. Also called target price or orientation price. It is one method of seeing whether a levy should be assessed, and how large it should be.

Gu

GUSHER
Flowing well, possibly not under control. Oil term.

HAIRCUT FINANCE
Loan against collateral in the US for less than the full value of the collateral, i.e. the loan is trimmed down.

HALF A BAR
Foreign exchange deal for half a million sterling.

HALF-LIFE
Period before half the principal of a bond issue is redeemed.

HAMMERED
Reference to a member of the Stock Exchange in the UK who cannot meet his debts. The defaulting member's name is posted on a board in the Stock Exchange showing those who have been expelled from the Exchange.

HARD CURRENCY
Strong currency, unencumbered by controls and easily exchangeable into other currencies.

HARDENING
A slowly advancing market, or a price which is stabilising.

HEAVY CRUDE
Crude oil with a high specific gravity but a low API gravity. See API.

HEDGE
Establishment of a position on a commodity futures market which is equal and opposite to a transaction made on an actual or physical market. It is also used in US stock and option markets.

HEDGING
Technique of minimising the risk of inventory loss or locking in a profit due to price fluctuations by taking equal and opposite positions in cash and futures.

HG

Heavy grain i.e. wheat, maize and rye.

HHDW

Handy heavy deadweight for highly compacted scrap metal. Shipping term.

HIRE PURCHASE

See INSTALMENT CREDIT.

HIRING RATE

See ACCESSION RATE.

H

HISTORIC COST

Original cost of a company's assets as distinct from replacement cost.

HIT THE BID

Dealer's willingness in the US to sell at the bid price or buy at the offer asked by another dealer.

HOARDING

Withdrawal of precious metals, coins and notes from active circulation for the purpose of accumulation without earning interest in anticipation of greater value, or profits in the future.

HOLDING COMPANY

Corporation or company controlling one or several companies through ownership of their stock, in most cases with voting control. Often used to bring together and supervise the interest of large corporations, or to facilitate diversification.

HOT MONEY

Sensitive short term speculative or arbitrage funds moving in very rapid response to exchange rate pressures or yield differentials.

Ho

HOT TREASURY BILLS
UK expression for treasury bills on the day they are issued with their full term to run.

HR
Hampton Roads: the areas on the US East Coast from where most US coal is exported. Shipping term.

HULL INSURANCE
Insurance of a ship, together with liabilities arising from collision etc.

HYDROCARBONS
Materials composed of hydrogen and carbon. They may be found as solids, liquids or gas. See PETROLEUM.

HYDROGENATION (COAL)
See COAL (HYDROGENATED).

HYPERBARIC CHAMBER
Chamber with a high internal pressure allowing divers to live under the same pressure conditions at which they work under water. A chamber in which divers work or are transported under water.

HYPERINFLATION
Rapidly climbing, self fuelling inflation which may bring on economic collapse.

HYPOTHECATION
(a) Letter of hypothecation allows a shipper to borrow from a bank using the vessel as security, but without giving the bank ownership of the security.
(b) In the US, pledging securities as collateral, i.e. to secure the debit balance on a margin account.

IADB

Inter-American Development Bank. Set up in 1959 to provide development funds for Central and Latin American countries. As well as these states, Japan and a large number of European countries are members.

IBEC

International Bank for Economic Co-operation. Established in 1964 to handle Comecon payments, especially transferable roubles. See COMECON.

IBRD

See WORLD BANK.

ICCH

International Commodities Clearing House. It operates a clearing system for the London Commodities Exchange as well as for the Australian Options Market, the Sydney Futures Exchange and the Hong Kong Commodity Exchange.

IDA

International Development Association. World Bank soft loan affiliate that lends on easy, concessionary terms to the poorest developing countries for specific development projects.

IEA

International Energy Agency. Formed after the 1973 oil crisis by the 21 leading western oil consuming nations to prevent another oil crisis. It is headquartered in Paris.

IFC

International Finance Corporation. World Bank affiliate, whose main function is to help private enterprises in developing countries, mobilising domestic and foreign capital, including its own, for this purpose.

IFP

Institut Français du Pétrole, des Carburants et Lubrifiants.

Ig

IGS

Inert gas systems. Used on oil tankers with tanks being filled with inert (non combustible) gas so as to prevent explosions. Shipping term.

ILO

International Labour Organisation. Its aim is to improve working conditions and social security throughout the world.

IMC

The International Monetary Conference organised by the American Bankers' Association. Holds an important annual conference on financial and monetary questions. Those attending must be the chairman or chief executive of the member bank.

IMF

International Monetary Fund. A specialised agency of the UN. It provides funds to member countries under certain conditions of need and commitments of policy. The fund was established by the Bretton Woods Agreement on a system of differential quota subscriptions representing drawing rights and voting power.

IMM

International Monetary Market. A division of the Chicago Mercantile Exchange (CME) for the trading of gold, foreign currencies and financial futures.

IMPORT COVER

Number of months of gross imports whose cost would be covered by a country's monetary reserves.

IMPORT DEPOSITS

Method of import restrictions requiring importers to deposit a percentage of the value of their imports for a set time before it is repaid.

IMPORT DUTY
Tariff or customs tax levied on goods crossing a national border. Import surcharge is an additional duty.

IMPORT LICENCE
Document authorising the importer to import the goods covered by the licence.

IMPORT RESTRICTIONS
Methods taken to reduce or control imports through a variety of measures including import deposits, licences or quotas. May be intended to correct a country's overall balance of payments deficit, or to protect a specific industrial sector.

INCOME BONDS
(a) In the UK fixed interest bonds provided by insurance companies; an immediate annuity.
(b) In the US bonds whose principal is guaranteed but on which interest payments are made only if earned and approved by the corporation's directors.

INCOME YIELD
In the UK the return over the next year in interest payments on a security.

INCOMES POLICY
Broad term covering the various direct forms of inflation control by a government which could include a freeze or limitation on increases in prices, wages, rents, dividends.

INCONVERTIBLE
Funds, currency or securities which cannot be freely converted into cash or another currency.

INDEMNITY
Guaranteed compensation against loss. Also security against contingent loss.

In

INDENTURE
Legal contract spelling out the obligations of a security issuer, and the rights of the holder of the security.

INDEPENDENT BROKER
Broker on the floor of the New York Stock Exchange who executes orders for other brokers or for firms without an exchange member on the floor.

INDEXATION (OR INDEXING)
System of linking wages, prices, interest rates, etc. to a given index, thus producing in the former an automatic rise or decline.

INDUSTRIAL PRODUCTION INDEX
Coincident indicator measuring the physical output of manufacturing, mining and utility industries.

INDUSTRIAL REVENUE BONDS
Bonds issued by US municipalities and used to sponsor industrial development. Some types are tax free.

INELIGIBLE BILLS
Bills which are not eligible for rediscount e.g. at the Bank of England or other central bank.

INERT
Resistant to chemical reaction with other substances.

INFANT INDUSTRY CLAUSE
Clause used to justify import tariff protection, especially in developing countries, where an industry in the early stages of development could collapse if faced with direct competition from imports.

INFLATION
Persistent upward movement in the general price level together with a related drop in purchasing power. Sometimes used to describe an excessive rate of such movement.

INFO RATE
Foreign exchange and money market term used when a dealer is providing a rate for information purposes only and not for doing business. Indicative or Indication Rate sometimes used for the same purpose.

INJECTION WELL
Used to inject gas or water into the reservoir to maintain pressure during secondary recovery or for conservation purposes.

INSIDER TRADING
Exploitation of inside or privileged information for profit in market transactions. More precisely in the US, trading on the basis of material non-public information gained through an insider or privileged position.

INSOLVENT
Being unable to pay debts as they become due; not strictly the same as BANKRUPTCY.

INSTALMENT CREDIT
Method of buying goods by paying the cost price plus a charge for credit by instalments. The purchase remains the property of the seller until the last instalment is paid, thus acting as security for the debt. In the UK it is known as hire purchase.

INSTITUTIONAL POT
In the US the share of a security offering specifically put aside for large institutional orders.

INSTRUMENT
Any type of financial debt paper.

INTANGIBLE ASSETS
Items such as the cost of patents and trade marks, the legal costs of purchasing or starting a business and goodwill.

In

INTERBANK
Market between banks for foreign exchange, Eurodeposits or domestic funds.

INTEREST ARBITRAGE
Switching funds between different interest bearing instruments or countries to profit from higher interest rates.

INTEREST COVER
Ability of a borrower to pay the interest payments due on a borrowing from currently available financial resourses.

INTEREST EQUALIZATION TAX
US tax introduced in 1963 and effectively lifted in 1974. Designed to discourage US citizens from purchasing certain securities issued in the US by taxing their income payments from such securities. A major factor in encouraging the emergence of the Eurobond market.

INTEREST PARITY
Occurs between two currencies when the differential in interest rates is directly reflected by the discount or premium in the forward exchange margins.

INTEREST PERIODS
Different interest rates and periods under a rollover credit which may be drawn down at different times.

INTEREST RATE
Charge, often annual, paid by a borrower to a lender over a period of time. It is intended to compensate a lender for the sacrifice of losing immediate use of money and for the inflationary erosion of its buying power over the life of a loan, and for the risk involved in lending the money. Interest rates are sensitively responsive to the supply and demand factors of credit and to inflationary expectations.

INTERIM COMMITTEE
Ministerial group in the IMF that deals with proposals to

reform the international monetary system. Its membership mirrors that of the IMF Board. Seven members are appointed by the US, Britain, France, West Germany, Japan, China and Saudi Arabia. The other 15 are elected by groups of countries usually in regional associations.

INTERIM DIVIDEND
Distribution of profits made by a company in a trading period, usually part-yearly e.g. quarterly, half-yearly. See FINAL DIVIDEND.

INTERMEDIATE GOODS
Goods used to produce other goods instead of being consumed themselves.

INTERMEDIATION
Opposite to disintermediation.

INTERNATIONAL BANK FOR RECONSTRUCTION AND DEVELOPMENT
See WORLD BANK

INTERNATIONAL CHAMBER OF COMMERCE (ICC)
Based in Paris this groups chambers of commerce, business and banking associations from around the world. It has an arbitration court used for settling international business disputes.

INTERNATIONAL DEBT ISSUE
Debt issue underwritten and sold outside the country of the borrower/guarantor. It may be a foreign bond issue or a Eurobond issue.

INTERNATIONAL DEPOSITARY RECEIPTS
See DEPOSITARY RECEIPT.

INTERNATIONAL INVESTMENT BANK
Set up in Moscow in 1971 to help finance development projects in the Comecon countries.

In

INTERNATIONAL MONETARY FUND
See IMF

INTERNATIONALISATION (OF CURRENCY)
A currency is internationalised if it is widely used to denominate trade and credit transactions by non-residents of the country of issue.

INTERVENTION
Central bank action in the open market to influence exchange rates, or to stabilise market conditions.

INTERVENTION PRICE
Within the EC, the delivered price paid for certain farm products under the EC Common Agricultural Policy for products accepted by an intervention agency at a specified centre. The product is required to meet minimum quality and quantity standards.

INTRA DAY LIMIT
Limits allowed on a foreign exchange dealer's position in each and all currencies during the course of the trading day. Such limits may well be substantially larger than those allowed at the close of business, when books are squared as far as possible.

INVERTED MARKET
Commodities futures market where the price of near months is higher than deferred months i.e. prices are inverted. Such a price structure normally reflects a shortage of supplies.

INVESTMENT
Employment of money in a purchase which is expected to produce an income or capital appreciation. Also anything which is purchased as a store of value.

INVESTMENT BANK
US bank acting as an underwriter for new issues of bonds or stocks and as part of a syndicate redistributes the issue to investors. Also carries out other functions similar to a British merchant bank.

INVESTMENT CURRENCY

Exchange control system under which currency needed for the acquisition of foreign investment must be acquired through an investment currency market, unless exempted by special permission from the central bank. If the investment currency meets strong demand, it will sell at a high premium over the actual foreign exchange market rate for the currency.

INVESTMENT TRUST (COMPANY)

Company engaged in buying securities of various kinds with a view to distributing the income to its shareholders.

INVISIBLE SUPPLY

Stocks (especially commodities) outside commercial channels whose exact quantity cannot be identified but which are in theory available to the market.

INVISIBLES

Exports and imports of services as opposed to trade in physical goods or merchandise. They form part of the current balance of payments component, and include funds arising from shipping, tourism, insurance, banking and commodity services.

INVITATION

Telex sent by a lead manager to prospective participants in a primary market issue especially Euromarket. It sets out conditions and asks whether they wish to participate.

IP

Institute of Petroleum. The official British organisation which deals with petroleum technology and with the standardisation of test methods for petroleum.

IRREDEEMABLES

British government stocks or debenture or loan stock, undated as to maturity and with no prospect of being paid off.

IRREVOCABLE CREDIT

Credit granted by a bank which cannot be revoked provided all the conditions are fulfilled.

Is

ISLAMIC DEVELOPMENT BANK
Based in Jeddah and set up in 1976, its role is to help finance development in countries with a substantial Islamic population.

ISOPACH MAP
Geological map giving the thickness of a particular stratum.

ISSUE
Offering of shares, stock or bonds.

ISSUE PRICE
Price at which securities are sold on issue. This is at face value or par, at a discount or at a premium. Occasionally an issue may be partly-paid meaning that the price at launch is met by instalments.

ISSUED CAPITAL
Portion of authorised capital actually issued in the form of common, ordinary or preferred stock.

ITF
International Transport Workers Federation. Ships' crews have to be members of the federation if the ships go to certain countries including Finland, Sweden, Australia, France and some UK ports.

IWL
Inside warranty limits. Refers to areas where ships can sail without hazards such as ice, icebergs.

'J' CURVE
Graphic description of the initially perverse and then benign reaction of the balance of trade following devaluation. The trade balance deteriorates as import costs rise, then recovers to surplus as exports expand in volume due to cheaper exchange costs.

Jo

JACKET PLATFORM
Platform constructed entirely of steel and normally kept in position by steel piles driven into the sea bed.

JACKUP RIG
Mobile offshore drilling platform with retractable legs on which the platform rests on the sea bed when in use.

JAMAICA AGREEMENT
Meeting of the IMF Interim Committee in 1976 which led to the abolition of the official gold price, and produced new rules and guidelines for the exchange rate regime moving from a system of fixed rates on which IMF rules were based to one allowing for flexibility.

J

JASON CLAUSE
Marine insurance term for risks which could not be discovered even if considerable care taken.

JAWBONE
Rhetoric by a government or other body to influence economic decisions by business, banking, consumers and trade unions, usually accompanied by forecasts, and sometimes by policy warnings.

JETTISONS
Goods thrown overboard to lighten a vessel.

JOB LOT
Trading unit which is smaller or larger than a full contract unit.

JOBBER
Wholesaler in securities on the London Stock Exchange.

JOBBER'S TURN
Difference between the price a jobber pays for the securities he deals in and the price he receives when reselling.

Jo

JOINT STOCK COMPANY
Incorporated or limited liability British bank or company. Recently retitled public limited company.

JUNIOR BONDS
In the US, bonds ranking lower in preference than other bonds.

JUNK BONDS
US high risk bonds issued by corporations rated in the lower categories of credit worthiness. The bonds are judged to have some speculative, as well as purely investment characteristics.

KELLY
Square or hexagonal hollow pipe which engages at one end with a drilling table and at the other with a drill pipe.

KENNEDY ROUND
Round of industrial tariff cuts in GATT between 1964 and 1967, so called because the initiative came from President Kennedy's Trade Expansion Act.

KERB
Trading outside official market hours.

KEROSENE
Medium-light distillate, used for lighting and heating, and to provide fuel for jet and turbo-prop aircraft engines; also spelt kerosine. In the UK called paraffin or paraffin oil.

KEYNESIAN ECONOMICS
Body of economic thought developed by John Maynard Keynes and his followers based on a cause and effect analysis of the variations in aggregate spending and income. It stands in opposition to the view that the free market is the ultimate regulator and believes that economic performance could be improved by government intervention.

130

KILLING A WELL

Overcoming the tendency of a well to flow naturally by filling the well bore with drilling mud or a similar substance.

KNOT

One nautical mile of 6,080 feet per hour. Normally used for shipping speed.

LABOUR FORCE

Total number of employed and registered or estimated unemployed persons in the economy. The unemployment rate or jobless ratio is a percentage of the civilian labour force.

LAFTA

Latin American Free Trade Area founded in 1960 with headquarters in Uruguay. Members are Argentina, Bolivia, Brazil, Chile, Colombia Ecuador, Mexico, Paraguay, Peru, Uruguay and Venezuela. Designed to promote trade liberalization. Due to be replaced by ALADI in 1983.

LAGGING INDICATOR

Measure of economic activity that usually reaches a turning point of the business cycle after the overall economy has turned, e.g. GNP, consumer prices, etc.

LAKEHEAD

Ports of Duluth, Superior and Thunder Bay in the Great Lakes. Shipping term.

LAKES FITTED

Vessel equipped to move through the Great Lakes with fenders fitted for passing through locks. It must not be more than 75 feet in width.

La

LANDED PRICE
Total cost of oil to a refiner, after accounting for all costs from site of production or purchase to the refinery.

LARGE TRADER
Trader who holds or controls a position in any one future of a commodity on any one contract market equal to or greater than the reporting level.

LASH
Lighter aboard ship. A system of carrying cargoes aboard ships in floating barges or lighters.

LAST NOTICE DAY
Final day for the issuing of notices of intent to deliver against a futures contract.

LAST TRADING DAY
Last day for trading in the current delivery month.

LAY BARGE
Barge built for laying submarine pipelines.

LAY DAYS
Specific period in days during which a ship must have arrived and be ready for loading operations under a charter party.

LAY OFF
To carry out a transaction offsetting a previous transaction and thus achieve a square or flat position.

LAY TIME
Maximum period during which a charterer can use a vessel for the purpose of loading and unloading cargoes without incurring financial liability known as demurrage.

LAY UP
To withdraw a vessel from trading and moor it semi-permanently at a specific location.

Le

L/D
Load/discharge. Shipping term.

LDCs
Less Developed Countries. Countries moving to a higher level of economic and social development. In general terms used to identify those countries which are not members of an established industrial grouping such as the OECD, G-10, COMECON.

LEAD MANAGER
Manager who leads a securities issue, e.g. Euroissue, and who is normally responsible for the contact with the borrower, organisation of the issue and preparation of the contracts and prospectus. He is also primarily responsible for putting together the issue syndicate (co-managers, underwriters), the selling group and for the placement of the issue. As a rule, the Lead Manager makes the largest commitment to take up and place bonds in the event of undersubscription. Also known as Lead Underwriter.

LEADING INDICATOR
Measure of economic activity in the business cycle that usually foreshadows peaks and troughs in total business, e.g.factory orders, stock prices.

LEADS AND LAGS
Accelerated and decelerated foreign trade payments and receipts, usually associated with exchange rate speculation. In anticipation of a devaluation, payments for exports are delayed while the importer accelerates his payments.

LEGAL LIST
List of investments in the US selected by various states in which certain institutions, banks and insurance companies are allowed to invest.

LEGAL TENDER
Means of payment which must be accepted by law in settlement of debt.

Le

LENDING MARGINS
Fixed spread which borrowers agree to pay above an agreed base rate, often Libor, to banks providing a Eurocredit. The total rate of interest paid by the borrower is adjusted, usually every six months, reflecting changes in Libor.

LEVERAGE
(a) Effect of the use of senior capital (bonds and preferred stock) over junior capital (common/ordinary stock) in capitalisations. High leverage can enable common/ordinary stockholders to benefit from an above-average level of profitability from employed loan stock, but it works to the company's detriment in a downturn since fixed charges must be met.
(b) In commodities indicates the margin/capital ratio.

LEVERAGED LEASE
Provision by lender of only a small share of the cost of equipment being leased, the rest being provided by a another lender.

LG
Light grains: barley and oats. Shipping term.

LIBERTY TYPE VESSEL
Built by the US during World War II and mostly multi-purpose cargo ships of about 15,000 dwt. They were tween-deckers. By the mid 1960s most had come to the end of their useful life and various countries started building Liberty replacements. The UK built SD 14s which it also had constructed under licence in Greece and Brazil. The Japanese built Freedom type vessels, and German Liberty Replacements were also built. These were all around 15,000 dwt. Some other types of replacement vessels have been constructed in various countries with sizes ranging from about 15,000 dwt to 22,000 dwt. These include the Santa Fe type vessels built in Spain of around 21,000 dwt.

LIBOR
London Interbank Offered Rate for Eurodollar funds, usually

three or six months, although it can range from overnight to five years. Different banks may quote differing Libor rates simply because they use different source banks. Information as to this rate is usually gathered in London at 1100 daily.

LICENCE BLOCK
Continental shelf section in a particular national sector bounded by latitude and longitude lines, usually at one-degree intervals. It is usually sub-divided further into smaller areas.

LICENSED WAREHOUSE
Warehouse approved by an exchange from which a commodity may be delivered under a futures contract.

LIFE
Period of time or term from a security's issue date to its maturity.

LIFE OF CONTRACT
Period between the beginning of trading in a particular futures contract and the expiration of trading.

LIFFE
London International Financial Futures Exchange.

LIFO
Last in, first out. See FIFO.

LIGHT CRUDE
Low specific gravity crude with high API gravity.

LIGHTERAGE
Price paid for loading or unloading ships by lighters or barges.

LIMIT
Maximum price fluctuation permitted in certain commodities or securities markets within any one session.

Li

LIMIT MOVE
Price that has advanced or declined the permissible limit during one trading session, as fixed by the rules of a contract or market.

LIMIT ORDER
Order in which the customer sets a limit on either price or time of execution, or both, as contrasted with a market order which implies the order be filled at the most favourable price as soon as possible. See also TIME ORDER.

LIMIT UP AND DOWN
Maximum price advance or decline from the previous day's settlement price permitted in one trading session.

LIMITED LIABILITY
Restriction of an owner's loss in a business to the amount of capital he has put into it.

LINER DISCHARGE
Shipowner pays for unloading and stevedores' wages.

LINER TERMS
Owner is responsible for arranging and paying for loading and discharging of ship.

LINK
(a) Relationship between trade and currency reform.
(b) Relationship between SDR allocations and development finance.

LIQUEFIED PETROLEUM GAS (LPG)
Light hydrocarbons from oil-bearing strata which are gaseous at normal temperatures, but which are liquefied by refrigeration or pressure to facilitate storage or transport. Mainly propane and butane.

LIQUID ASSETS
Also quick assets. Cash and readily disposable current assets.

LIQUIDATE
To close out a long position in government securities and other assets, including commodity futures. Closing a short position is usually called covering.

LIQUIDATION
(a) Dissolution or winding up of a company, either voluntary or compulsory.
(b) Disposal of assets for cash.

LIQUIDITY
(a) Cash, or cash position, or international money supply.
(b) Depth of a market (e.g. securities or commodities) and its ability to absorb sudden shifts in supply and demand without excessive price fluctuation.

LIQUIDITY RATIOS
Ratios which indicate a borrower's ability to meet short term obligations incurred. The ratio of liquid assets to current liabilities is described as the quick or acid test ratio on a company's balance sheet.

LIQUID MARKET
Market where selling and buying can be accomplished with ease.

LISTING
When a securities issue is listed on a stock exchange it is approved for trading.

LISTS CLOSED
A list of applications to subscribe to an issue of securities is closed on a set date by those making the issue.

LLOYDS
The Corporation of Lloyds in London and the associated insurance market, where virtually any insurance proposal may be accepted for underwriting.

L1

LLOYDS REGISTER
Annual alphabetical list of commercial vessels of more than 100 tons on a worldwide basis classified according to seaworthiness. Published in London.

LME
London Metals Exchange.

LOA
Length overall of a vessel. Shipping term.

LOAN CAPITAL
Part of a company's capital represented by loans from outside the company.

LOAN PROGRAMME
Means by which the US government provides price support by lending money to farmers at preannounced rates with the farmers' crop used as collateral.

LOAN STOCK
Long term interest bearing stock issued by a company, often as a debenture.

LOCAL AUTHORITY
British municipal governing bodies whose deposits and loans comprise an important secondary money market in London.

LOCK GATE
EC agricultural minimum import price based on the theoretical CIF price for certain farm product imports.

LOCKED IN
A situation where an investor has made a profit on the purchase of a commodity or security, and finds his potential profit reduced if he disposes of the security or commodity, e.g. through imposition of a capital gains tax.

LOMBARD RATE

Rate at which a central bank provides loans to banks secured against first class paper.

LOMÉ CONVENTION

Agreement between the EC and a number of developing countries in Africa, the Caribbean and the Pacific. Covers trade preferences and development assistance.

LONG HEDGE

Buying of futures contracts in expectation of actual cash market purchases.

LONG INTEREST

Long holdings or contracts in any given futures markets.

LONG POSITION

Situation in which a commodity, currency or security has been bought on a net basis and should be cancelled out by a corresponding sale.

LONG TERM CAPITAL ACCOUNT

Balance of payments term to distinguish investment and government expenditure and receipts abroad from short term capital or hot money flows. Together with the current account it forms the basic balance of payments.

LONG THE BASIS

Person or firm buying a spot commodity and hedging with a sale of futures is 'long the basis'.

LONG TON

Ton of 2,240 lbs.

LONGS

British government stocks with a maturity exceeding 15 years.

Lo

LOT

The unit of trading especially in commodities. More or less than the standard unit is described as an odd or job lot.

LUMP SUM

Amount paid for chartering a vessel for an agreed capacity instead of the more usual per ton basis.

LUXIBOR

Luxembourg Interbank Offered Rate.

LWT

Lightweight tons. Weight of steel in a ship, usually quoted when a ship is sold for scrap, when the price is given in dollars per light ton.

M1/M2/M3/M4/M5

See MONEY SUPPLY.

MACRO-ECONOMICS

Study of human activities in large groups as indicated by economic aggregates such as total employment, national income, investment, consumption, prices, wages, costs.

MAGNETOMETER SURVEY

Geological survey identifying sedimentary basins by measuring the magnetic properties of the underlying igneous rocks.

MAINTENANCE MARGIN

Margin normally less than, but still part of, the original margin which must be maintained on deposit at all times.

MAIZE

European term interchangeable with the US corn.

MAKE A MARKET
See MARKET MAKER.

MAKE UP DAY
Day when bank figures, must be compiled for reporting to the central bank.

MANAGED FLOAT
Currency float subject to guidance by discretionary central bank intervention. Also called a dirty float, when intervention is deemed to delay unnecessarily needed government action, i.e. a devaluation/revaluation, wage freeze.

MANAGEMENT COMMITTEE (EC)
Comprises EC national agricultural ministry experts and commodity specialists for farm product groups subject to EC price support.

M

MANAGEMENT FEE
(a) Charge by banks for managing a securities issue or credit, especially on Euromarkets.
(b) Fee paid to the operators of an investment company.

MANAGEMENT GROUP
Group of financial institutions which co-ordinate closely with the lead manager in the distribution and pricing of an issue.

MANDATE
Formal authority to a banker setting out a customer's instructions, e.g. a lead manager is given a mandate to raise funds for a client.

MANDATORY REDEMPTION
Feature of certain security or debt issues, involving the obligatory redemption by the issuer of part of the issue before full maturity through the operation of a sinking fund.

Ma

MANIFEST

Detailed list of cargo carried aboard a vessel or plane.

MANMADE FIBRES

Industrially produced fibres as opposed to natural fibres such as cotton and wool. Includes both artificial and synthetic fibres.

MARGIN

Incremental percentage referring to deposits, collateral or permissible exchange rate fluctuations.

(a) In commodities it is the amount of money or collateral deposited with a broker, or with the clearing house, to insure against loss on open futures contracts. It is not a part payment on a purchase. Maintenance margin is the amount which must be maintained on deposit with the broker at all times.

(b) A method of quoting forward exchange rates.

(c) In stock markets shares may be bought 'on margin', the buyer having to pay only part of the purchase price in cash immediately, i.e. the customer uses his broker's credit.

MARGIN CALL

If a commodity futures or securities market moves against a trader or speculator he may receive a margin call to provide extra finance or security, to maintain his margin.

MARGIN REQUIREMENTS

(a) Incremental reserve obligations on credit instruments.

(b) In the US, the percentage of reserves required by the Federal Reserve and exchanges to make an initial credit transaction or maintain a margin account.

MARGINAL FIELD

Oil or gas field whose development depends on whether it will generate enough net income at a given time. It may later become commercial, if conditions change.

MARINE RISER
Pipe linking a marine exploration rig, drilling platform or production platform to an undersea wellhead or subsea pipeline during drilling or production operations.

MARK OR MARKING
In the London Stock Market a price given in the Daily Official List under the heading Business Done at which a transaction took place on the previous day.

MARKER PRICE
OPEC oil benchmark price based on Saudi Arabia's Arabian Light 34° API crude oil.

MARKET ACCESS
(a) Scope for access to a country's markets available to imported goods or commodities.
(b) Access to a market for executing transactions.

MARKET AMOUNT
Amount normally considered the minimum for dealings in a market, especially foreign exchange.

MARKET FORCES
Conditions of supply and demand which operate in a free market to determine prices through the decisions of buyers and sellers, lenders and borrowers.

MARKET MAKER
Recognised financial institution or individual making consistent buy and sell quotations in a selection of issues in the secondary market. A principal requisite is that the market maker must hold or have ready access to the issues quoted, i.e. carry an inventory.

MARKET ORDER
Order to buy or sell a security or a futures contract at the best price obtainable at the time it is entered in the market.

Ma

MARKET PARTICIPANT
One who buys and sells on behalf of clients and on his own account.

MARKET POSITION
The supply and demand relationship of a given security at a given price.

MARKET TREND
General direction, ignoring short term fluctuations of price movements in the market.

MARKET VALUE
Current trading price of a commodity, security or currency, and the level at which it can be bought or sold. Also the value of fixed assets e.g. plant and equipment.

MARKETABILITY
Measure of ease with which something can be bought and sold.

MATCH
Two offsetting transactions either on a dealer's own account or for one or more customers.

MATCHED BOOK
A situation where the maturity dates for a bank's or trader's liabilities match those of his assets.

MATCHED SALE-PURCHASE AGREEMENT
Outright sale of a security by the US Federal Reserve for immediate delivery to a dealer or a foreign central bank, with an agreement to buy back the security on a specific date, usually seven days, at the same price. Such agreements enable the Federal Reserve to withdraw reserves on a temporary basis from the banking system.

MATURITY
Life of a bond/loan. The period within which a futures

contract can be settled by the delivery of the actual commodity.

MATURITY DATE

Delivery or settlement date for a futures contract. Final redemption date for a bond/loan.

MAXIMUM/MINIMUM PRICE FLUCTUATION

Maximum or minimum movement allowed in the price of a futures contract in a trading session. In the US, minimum fluctuation is the smallest permissible price change in a given contract.

MBT

Motor blocks and turnings. Shipping term.

MCA

See MONETARY COMPENSATION AMOUNT.

MEDIUM TERM FORECASTS

Economic predictions ranging from seven quarters to four years ahead of the current period.

MEDIUMS

British government stocks with a life of between 5 and 15 years.

MEMBERS RATE

Commission charged for executing an order on behalf of an exchange member.

MERCHANT BANK

Originally a bank which specialised in financing international trade and as such developed specialist knowledge of the countries with which it dealt. Now plays a much broader role by acting as an issuing house for stocks, bonds, by raising loans, equity capital, dealing in bills and foreign exchange. Merchant banks also act for and advise companies, e.g. in merger situations, and some deal in bullion.

Me

MERGER
Fusion of two companies or, sometimes, an acquisition or a takeover of one company by another.

METHANE
Odourless inflammable gas which forms an explosive mixture with air.

METHANOL
Methyl alcohol—a colourless, poisonous liquid with a faint smell—used to mix with petrol to help power vehicles.

METRE
3.28084275 feet. A cubic metre equals 35.3148 cubic feet.

METRIC TON (TONNE)
2204.6223 lbs.

MICRO-ECONOMICS
Study of the economic action of individual firms and well-defined small groups of individuals and sectors.

MILO
US term for grain sorghum.

MINIMUM LENDING RATE
See MLR

MINIMUM RESERVES
Minimum amount of reserves which commercial banks and other depository institutions are required to keep on deposit with a central bank. Sometimes called Registered Reserves.

MINORITY INTEREST
Equity interest in a subsidiary company which is held outside the controlling parent company.

MINORITY SHAREHOLDERS
Holders of the minority interest in a subsidiary company.

Mo

MIT
>Market if touched. A commodity order to sell/buy at a specific price.

MLR
>Minimum Lending Rate. British bank rate. The minimum rate at which the Bank of England used to lend to the discount market. From August 20 1981, kept in reserve to be used only in exceptional circumstances when strong guidance is needed to change the direction of interest rates.

MOL
>More or less. Shipping term.

MONETARISM
>School of economic thought which advocates strict control of the money supply as the major weapon of monetary policy, especially against inflation. Usually involves cuts in public spending and temporarily high interest rates.

MONETARY BASE
>Monetary aggregate consisting of money held by the banks and the public plus bank deposits with the central bank. Expansion of the monetary base is said to determine the potential growth rate of the money stock.

MONETARY COMPENSATION AMOUNT (MCA)
>Border adjustment used to even out the difference between green currencies and the actual foreign exchange value of EC currencies. It is calculated weekly. The MCA acts as a subsidy on food imports for a country with a weak currency, since it brings prices down from the high green currency level to the lower foreign exchange or real value. By the same token, it makes farm exports from such countries dearer. For countries with strong currencies, exports are cheaper and imports dearer but it also ensures prices paid to farmers in those countries do not fall. See GREEN CURRENCY

Mo

MONETARY POLICY
Management by a central bank of a country's money supply to ensure the availability of credit in quantities and at prices consistent with specific national objectives.

MONETARY REFORM
Process of negotiating and drafting a revised international currency system.

MONEY MARKET
Series of homogeneous national credit and deposit markets involving short term securities and operated by the central bank, the commercial banks and financial institutions.

MONEY SUPPLY
Most narrowly defined (M1), the money stock consists of cash and sight (demand in the US) deposits with banks. Broader definitions (M2, M3, M4) add in various categories of time and savings deposits and certificates of deposit until the broadest definition (M5) includes all that can be deemed 'money' in the short, medium and long term.

MONTHLY INCREMENTS
EC term describing the monthly increases in intervention, target and threshold prices intended to provide compensation for storage and help orderly product marketing.

MOODY'S
US firm which, along with Standard & Poor's, operates a bond rating system from 'triple A' to 'C', for both corporate and municipal credits.

MORATORIUM
A situation where a borrower makes a formal statement that he is unable to meet all or part of his debts. It is usually a holding action designed to lead to re-negotiation of outstanding debt repayments. Not to be confused with default.

MOST FAVOURED NATION
Tariff privileges accorded by a nation to any other which are extended to others with which it has treaties awarding MFN treatment.

MULTICURRENCY
A loan or bond issue involving several currencies. A bond issue may be made in a specific currency but repayable in several. A rollover credit may be made available in different currencies to suit the borrower.

MULTINATIONAL
Company that has manufacturing bases or other forms of direct investment in several countries.

MULTIPLE EXCHANGE RATE
Use by a country of several exchange rates for different operations. Thus foreign investment, foreign tourists and raw material imports, may be given a cheaper rate, while imports of non-essentials are charged a higher rate of foreign exchange.

MULTIPLES
Analytical equity ratios such as price/earnings ratio; a corporation stock price expressed as a multiple of reported earnings per share.

MULTIPLIER
Conceptual tool referring to the magnified impact that investment and spending have on total income, or that reserve requirements have on bank positions.

MUNICIPAL BOND
Bond issued by a state, local or government authority especially in the US. The interest is exempt from US federal taxation. The two major categories are General Obligation Bonds and Reserve Bonds.

Mu

MUTUAL FUND
Open-end investment company i.e. one which continuously sells and redeems its shares. These shares are not traded on any exchange.

NAKED POSITION
Unhedged long or short position.

NAPOLEON
French 20 gold franc coin.

NARROWER BANDS
Tighter exchange rate fluctuation margins than applied as a matter of standard international practice.

NASD
National Association of Security Dealers, a self regulatory US body.

NASDAQ SYSTEM
National Association of Securities Dealers Automated Quotations. A computerised quotation system for issues quoted on the US Over the Counter (OTC) market, sponsored by NASD. See OTC.

NATIONAL DEBT
Total indebtedness of a national government as a result of cumulative net budget deficits. Normally financed by the sale of different categories of government securities and debt instruments.

NATIONALISM (OF CURRENCY)
This occurs when a central bank imposes restrictions on borrowing and lending of its currency by non-residents.

Ne

NATURAL GAS
Mixture of light hydrocarbons (predominantly methane) frequently found in association with oil.

NB
A newly built vessel. Shipping term.

NEARBYS
Nearest delivery months of a commodity futures contract.

NEGATIVE PLEDGE
An undertaking by a borrower not to raise new loans giving new creditors preferential terms over existing creditors. Can also apply to the re-negotiation of existing loans.

NEGOTIABLE CDs
See CERTIFICATE OF DEPOSIT.

NEGOTIABLE ORDER OF WITHDRAWAL (NOW ACCOUNT)
Interest earning account in the US on which technically only bank drafts may be drawn. In practice virtually a cheque account. May be owned only by individuals and certain non-profit organisations.

NEGOTIATED SALE
Issue of securities in which the price and other terms of sale are set by the securities underwriters and issuer through negotiations. The opposite is a competitive sale where sealed bids are submitted.

NET ASSET WORTH
Measurement of value applied to ordinary shares and calculated by dividing the net equity assets by the number of ordinary shares.

Ne

NET BORROWED RESERVES
Margin by which borrowings from US Federal Reserve banks outweigh excess reserves.

NET CASH FLOW
Retained earnings plus depreciation.

NET CHANGE
Change in the price between the close on one day and the closing price on the following day in which the stock, currency or commodity is traded.

NET EQUITY ASSETS
Net assets less the repayment value of the preference capital including any arrears of interest.

NET LIQUIDITY BALANCE
US Department of Commerce term describing the overall balance of payments.

NET POSITION
Difference between the open long contracts and open short contracts held in any one commodity on a futures market.

NET PROFIT
Trading profits after deducting the charges detailed in the profit and loss account. These include debits such as taxation, depreciation, auditors' and directors' fees.

NET WORKING CAPITAL
Current assets net of current liabilities.

NET WORTH
Total assets net of total liabilities. Equivalent to capital.

NEW MONEY

In a refunding operation, the amount by which the nominal value of the securities is greater than that of the maturing securities. Thus, the borrower takes in additional cash beyond the amount being repaid.

NEW TIME DEALING

Dealing for 'new time' on the London Stock Exchange during the two days preceding the next accounting period. This enables payment for the deal to be deferred until the settlement day of the following account.

NEW YORK COMMODITY EXCHANGE INC

Commodity futures market trading principally in gold, silver and copper.

NO PAR VALUE

Stocks without face, or nominal, value.

NOLA

New Orleans. Shipping term.

NOMINAL PRICE

Estimated price quoted in the absence of actual transactions, normally an average between the last bid and the last offer.

NON-DURABLES

See SOFT GOODS.

NON O/A

Not over age. When a charterer does not want a vessel more than 15 years old. Shipping term.

NON-RESIDENT ACCOUNT

Account owned by a person who is not a resident of the country where the account is held.

No

NOSTRO ACCOUNT
Bank's account held with a foreign bank, e.g. a US bank's account in Germany with a German bank. See VOSTRO ACCOUNT.

NOTE
In the US one of a range of debt securities. US Treasury notes refer to coupon securities with a maturity of one to ten years, while municipal notes are short term promissory notes.

NOTE ISSUE
Amount of bank notes issued by the issuing authority.

NOTICE DAY
Day on which notices of intent to deliver on futures contracts may be issued.

NRT
Net register tons. This is the part of a ship's gross register tons considered for cargo. It is the gross tonnage less the machinery, boiler and bunker, crew and stores spaces.

NSCC
US National Securities Clearing Corporation set up in 1977 by the merger of clearing facilities owned by the New York and American Stock Exchanges and the National Clearing Corporation for the National Association of Securities Dealers.

NYFCC
New York Futures Clearing Corp set up by New York Futures Exchange to handle clearing operations.

NYFE
New York Futures Exchange established in August 1979 and a wholly owned subsidiary of the New York Stock Exchange.

NYSE
The New York Stock Exchange.

Od

NYSE COMMON STOCK INDEX
Composite index covering all stocks listed on the Big Board, based on the market close at end December 1965 as 50.00 and weighted according to the number of shares listed for each issue. There are four supplementary indices for industrials, transportation, utilities and finance.

OAPEC – ORGANISATION OF ARAB PETROLEUM EXPORTING COUNTRIES
Set up in 1968. Its members are Algeria, Bahrain, Iraq, Kuwait, Libya, Qatar, Saudi Arabia, Syria and the United Arab Emirates. Egypt was suspended in 1979. It is an association separate from the oil price fixing and Vienna-based OPEC.

OBLIGATORY WELLS
Wells drilled in a given area as a condition for receiving an exploration licence.

OBO
Ore/bulk/oil carrier. Shipping term.

OBU
Offshore Banking Unit. A foreign bank usually handling foreign exchange, Eurocurrency and domestic money market transactions in a centre where the capital market is free and enjoys advantages in terms of tax and/or reserve requirements.

ODD DATES
Deals in foreign exchange and money markets for periods other than the regular market periods.

ODD LOT
Trading lot in a quantity or amount smaller or larger than the regular market lot.

O

155

Oe

OECD

See ORGANISATION FOR ECONOMIC CO-OPERATION AND DEVELOPMENT.

OFFERED MARKET

When offers outnumber bids in a given market or for a given security.

OFFERED RATE

Rate at which a bank or dealer is prepared to do business.

OFFICIAL JOURNAL

The Journal of the European Communities containing EC regulations, budgets, directives, decisions, opinions and recommendations.

OFFICIAL SETTLEMENTS ACCOUNT

Also called reserves transactions account. A US balance of payments measure based on movements of dollars in foreign official holdings and in US reserves.

OFFSHORE CENTRE (MARKET)

Conglomeration of OBUs drawn together by the tax advantages of operating in that centre. Examples: Bahrain, Cayman Islands, Philippines.

OIL TRAP

Hydrocarbon retained by a geological structure. This results in the formation of an oil field.

O/O

Ore/oil carrier. Shipping term.

OPEC – ORGANISATION OF PETROLEUM EXPORTING COUNTRIES

Formed in 1960, its members are Algeria, Ecuador, Gabon, Indonesia, Iran, Iraq, Kuwait, Libya, Nigeria, Qatar, Saudi Arabia, United Arab Emirates and Venezuela. It controls around half the world's oil trade and sets an official price for crude oil which may dictate world price levels.

OPEN END

See MUTUAL FUND.

OPEN MARKET

Central bank sale or purchase of securities intended to influence the volume of money and credit in the economy. Chiefly involves short term government securities, but also medium and long term securities. Purchases inject reserves into the system thus expanding credit while sales have the opposite effect.

OPEN MARKET COMMITTEE

See FEDERAL OPEN MARKET COMMITTEE.

OPEN OUTCRY

Method of public auction required for making bids and offers in some commodity markets and stock markets.

OPEN POSITION (OPEN INTEREST)

Total of futures contracts open at any one time which have not yet been matched and closed by a corresponding opposite transaction, i.e. there has been no subsequent sale or purchase, nor has delivery been made or taken of the financial instrument or physical commodity. Also called Open Contracts or Open Commitments.

OPERATOR

Person or legal entity with authority to drill wells and undertake production if hydrocarbons are discovered; may drill wells himself or employ a drilling contractor to do so. Frequently the operator is part of a consortium, and may act on behalf of the consortium.

OPTION

Right, acquired for a price, to buy certain specified property, e.g. a security or an instrument, or to sell at an agreed price within a specified time.

Or

ORDINARY CAPITAL

Capital in a company which is entitled to the residue (or equity) of profits and assets after senior capital issues, such as preference or preferred ordinary shares, as well as creditors and others outside the business have received their due.

ORDINARY DIVIDEND

Part of the profit accruing to the ordinary capital which is distributed to its holders. In the US also called common dividend.

ORDINARY SHARES

See ORDINARY CAPITAL.

ORGANISATION FOR ECONOMIC COOPERATION AND DEVELOPMENT (OECD)

Established in 1961 to promote stable and sustainable economic growth in member countries and the expansion of world trade. Consists of 24 countries and groups: the US, Canada, Japan, Australia and New Zealand, all EC and EFTA member states as well as Iceland, Spain and Turkey. Yugoslavia is an associate member. An important forum for the discussion of economic policies of member states. It publishes a regular review of each country. Based in Paris.

ORIGINAL MATURITY

Time to maturity of a security at the date on which it was issued.

OTC (OVER THE COUNTER)

OTC market differs from organised US stock exchanges in its transactions. These are conducted nationally, by telephone and telex, directly between dealers as principals rather than agents, and not on a localised highly regulated trading floor.

OVER AGE

A vessel more than 15 years old although occasionally can refer to a vessel more than 20 years. Additional insurance is charged on an over age vessel. Shipping term.

OVERAGE
Extra cargo which a tanker may have the option to carry in addition to a part cargo already fixed. Shipping term.

OVER-ALLOCATION
Situation where lead managers of bond issues allocate to the selling group a larger sum of bonds than is actually planned for issue.

OVERBOUGHT
Situation where rates or prices of a currency, commodity or security may have advanced too far in response to net buying pressure, thus creating a vulnerable market.

OVERHANG
Involuntary foreign official holdings of a currency, usually a generalised condition, i.e. relating to a large number of countries and involving historically large amounts of the currency concerned net of working balances. The overhang represents in these circumstances temporary inconvertibility due to the inability of the reserve currency country to convert the overhang into other forms of acceptable reserve asset.

OVERNIGHT
Deal from the current trading day to the next. At weekends, this means Friday to Monday.

OVERSOLD
Opposite to OVERBOUGHT.

OVERSUBSCRIBED
Issue of securities when applications to buy are in excess of available shares, units etc. Opposite of UNDERSUB-SCRIBED.

OVERVALUED
Situation where market and economic conditions and pressures indicate a currency should be devalued. Opposite to UNDERVALUED.

Pa

P & S

Purchase and sale statement in the US showing the customer's net ledger balance with a broker after the offset of a previously established position.

PADDY

Also Padi. Rough or harvested RICE which has not been husked or processed.

PAID UP CAPITAL

Part of the issued capital for which the nominal value has been received by the company and on which no further liabilities attach to the shareholders.

PAID UP SHARES

Shares for which the company has received the full nominal value in payment.

PALLION VESSEL

A vessel of around 17,000 long dwt built at the Pallion ship-yard in the UK.

PANAMAX SIZE

Vessel which can move through the Panama Canal. Usually means a vessel below 65,000 long dwt.

PAPER

General term for securities, commercial paper, money market instruments etc., especially short term.

PAPER PROFIT

Apparent profit arising out of an unrealised increase in the value of an asset.

PAR

Price of a security when this is equal to its nominal, or face, value. Has more significance with bonds indicating maturity risk, than it has with common stock.

PARAFFIN

Term given in the UK the top grade of kerosene used in lamps and space heaters.

PARIS

Foreign exchange term for the French franc.

PARITY

Officially declared exchange rate in terms of SDR, gold or the US dollar. Also called Par Value.

PART CARGO

Acceptance by a shipowner of a charter under which the ship will not be fully loaded and unused space is not paid for.

PARTICIPATING PREFERENCE CAPITAL

Capital whose holders are entitled not only to the receipts of a fixed interest payment out of profits but also, in certain defined circumstances, to a share in the balance of the profits.

PARTICIPATION FEE

Fee charged by a bank for taking part in providing a loan, e.g. in the Euromarket.

PARTICULAR AVERAGE LOSS

Damage caused to a particular cargo, with the loss borne by the insurers of that cargo alone.

PARTLY PAID

Shares for which the full nominal value has not been paid and on which a liability to pay the balance exists. Often used in connection with new issues when the terms of the issue require only part of the issue price to be paid on application.

PASSING DIVIDEND

No dividend payments authorised by a company due to a lack of, or insufficient, profits.

Pa

PAY ZONE

Layer of rock in which oil and/or gas is found. Pay sand describes a sand reservoir containing gas and oil.

PAYDOWN

Amount by which, in a US Treasury refunding, the par value of maturing securities is greater than that of those being sold.

PAYING AGENT

Bank of a bond issuer where principal and interest are payable.

PAYUP

Difference in cost between selling a securities block, and then buying another more expensive block.

PC

Part cargo. Shipping term.

P/E RATIO

Price/earnings ratio. The current market price of a company's stock expressed as a multiple of its total per share earnings for the previous 12 months.

PEGGING

Term used to describe end of a currency float and the setting of a fixed central rate or parity. Also REPEGGING.

PENSION FUNDS

Funds invested by the state, trade union or corporate sector for their members' pensions. An important source of finance for the capital market and investment. Pension funds can have a considerable impact on stock markets, as well as on economic activity.

PERCENTAGE EARNINGS

Profit expressed as a percentage of the nominal capital employed.

PERFORMANCE BOND
Instrument aimed at ensuring a service or contract is completed correctly. If this is not the case, then the bank issuing or guaranteeing the bond will be required to make a compensatory payment.

PETROCHEMICAL
Chemical substance derived from petroleum or natural gas, e.g. ethylene, propylene, benzene, and toluene.

PETRODOLLARS
Surplus funds resulting from oil sales for dollars available by oil producing countries, especially OPEC.

PETROLEUM
Mixture of hydrocarbons and other organic compounds. It includes natural gas liquids, natural gas and related products.

PH
Per hatch. Loading or discharging is often given as so many tons per hatch per day. Shipping term.

PHD
Per hatch per day. Shipping term.

PHYSICALS
Actual commodities as opposed to futures contracts. See ACTUALS.

PICKUP
Yield gain occurring when a block of securities is sold, followed by the purchase of a higher yielding block.

PIG
Object placed in pipeline and propelled by gas or oil flow to clean, clear or check the internal condition of the pipeline.

Pi

PIT

Area on a trading floor where futures contract trading takes place. Also called ring.

PL 480

See PUBLIC LAW 480.

PLACING

See PRIVATE PLACEMENT.

PLACING POWER

Ability of a financial institution to place newly issued securities with investors.

PLANNED ECONOMY

Economy where distribution of resources is centrally controlled by government.

PLATFORM

Offshore structure enabling development wells to be drilled.

PLIMSOLL LINE

Water level on British registered vessels which indicates the maximum permitted loading level. Shipping term.

PLOUGHED BACK PROFIT (EARNINGS)

Profit which is not distributed but reinvested in the company.

PLUGGING

Sealing of well which is no longer, and not likely to be, needed.

PLUS ACCRUED INTEREST

Applied to the price of bonds with interest accruing from the date of the last payment. A seller is therefore entitled to receive the interest, as calculated from the last interest date to the business day following the day on which the sale is made, from the buyer.

PMO

Passing Muscat outbound. Muscat is a port in the Sultanate of Oman. Shipping term.

POINT

Used in describing changes in stock/bond prices or exchange and interest rates. e.g. in the US stock market one point equals one dollar, while in the bond market it is equal to 10 dollars. See BASIS PQINT.

PORE PRESSURE

Original pressure in a rock formation.

PORK BELLIES

Part of a hog carcass producing bacon.

POROSITY

Measure of the amount of gaps or voids in a rock; normally recorded as a percentage of the overall volume.

POSITION

(a) Client's status on the securities or commodities market as represented by unliquidated long or short open contracts.
(b) Commodity in a convenient position for delivery or shipment is termed 'in position'.

POSITION LIMIT

Maximum position, either net long or net short, in one commodity futures or all futures of a single commodity which may be held or controlled by a single person under CFTC or exchange rules. It has a similar meaning regarding listed options.

POSSIBLE RESERVES

Oil and/or gas reserves which the best estimates suggest might eventually be recoverable from undrilled or untested structures, but which have not yet been developed.

Po

POSTED PRICE
Hypothetical price level for crude oil on which OPEC governments based their 'take' from foreign producing companies in the form of taxes and royalties. No longer in wide use.

POTENTIAL GNP
Output that an economy can produce when operating at full employment capacity.

POTENTIAL TEST
Test which provides information on the productive capacity of a well.

POUR POINT
Pour point of petroleum is the lowest temperature at which the oil will pour or flow when it is chilled under prescribed conditions.

POWER OF ATTORNEY
Legal document authorising one person to act for another either for a specific time and/or purpose or in general.

PP
Picked ports, i.e. selected ports. Shipping term.

PRE-EMPTIVE RIGHT
Right of shareholders and others to maintain their proportional control of, and equity in a corporation when additional shares are issued.

PREFERENTIAL DEBTS
If a company is being wound up debts are classified as secured and unsecured. In both cases certain creditors have a preference over the others.

PREFERRED STOCK/SHARES
Fixed dividend shares which have a prior asset claim over common stock/shares. Ordinary or common shareholders

cannot receive dividends until preferred dividends have been paid in full.

PREMIUM

A margin paid above the normal price level. It may reflect market conditions. Near delivery and higher quality can put one futures contract at a premium over another. Also the amount by which a bond sells above par.

PRESHIPMENT FINANCE

Covers an exporter's costs before shipment of goods.

PRESSURE BURST

Sudden bursting of rock due to great pressure in deep mining.

PRICE LIMIT

Maximum permitted advance or decline in a market during a trading session. Also the specified price in a limit order. In the futures market limits are set by the exchanges and can be altered depending on market volatility.

PRIMARY COMMODITIES

Commodities in the raw or unprocessed state, e.g. natural rubber, iron ore.

PRIMARY MARKET

(a) Market for the placing of securities such as international, domestic and foreign bond issues and stock with investors by the group organised to handle the issue. The sale proceeds go to the issuer and not to other investors. Any subsequent resale or purchase is handled on the secondary market.
(b) Market for the sale or shipment of primary commodities.

PRIMARY RESERVES

Gold-related monetary reserves, i.e. gold, SDR, reserve position in the IMF.

Pr

PRIME RATE
Theoretically lowest loan interest rate charged by US banks to their best-rated corporate customers.

PRINCIPAL
(a) Face amount of a bond, exclusive of accrued interest.
(b) Person employing another to act as agent, a person acting for his own account in a transaction.

PRIOR CHARGES
Charges on debentures, loan stock, notes etc. which rank ahead of share capital. The service of interest on such charges is a cost of running the company which must be met before any dividend is paid, and in the event of default on the conditions of the issue the repayment of such indebtedness is a charge ranking before share capital.

PRIOR IMPORT DEPOSITS
Import deposits which need to be paid before an import licence is granted.

PRIORITY PERCENTAGE
Apportionment of profit earned in any year which is required to service the different classes of capital expressed, in order of priority, as a percentage of the amount available.

PRIVATE PLACEMENT
New issue, in the form of stock or debt which has essentially been placed with a selected group, e.g. institutional investors, rather than offered to the market by an underwriting syndicate. In the US these offerings are not subject to SEC registration requirements.

PRODUCTIVITY
Output per man-hour or unit of capital.

PROFIT MARGIN
Net profit as a percentage of sales or capital.

PROLERISED SCRAP
Scrap metal which has been broken up. Shipping term.

PROMISSORY NOTE
Written promise to pay, used as an instrument of commodity futures trading and of direct company borrowing in the form of commercial paper.

PROMPT
Term applied to a vessel able to arrive at a required loading port within a few days.

PROSPECTUS
Document offering and giving details of a new issue of stock or debt.

PROTECTIONISM
Imposition of border taxes (customs duties) on imports in order to protect a domestic industry from cheaper competitive products.

PROTECTIONISM (OF CURRENCY)
Central bank system to protect currency with restrictions in order to move the exchange rate in a direction consistent with the economic policies of the government concerned.

PROXY
Person or legal entity authorised to represent, and if necessary act and vote on behalf of another.

PSBR
See PUBLIC SECTOR BORROWING REQUIREMENT.

PUBLIC ELEVATORS
Grain elevators in the US used for the bulk storage of grains. Some elevators are approved delivery points for grain under futures contracts.

PUBLIC LAW 480
Also known as the food for peace programme. The main US legislative authority for providing food and farm product aid

to developing countries, in the form of outright donation or on long term credit at low interest. Enacted in 1954 as the Agricultural Trade Development and Assistance Act.

PUBLIC SECTOR BORROWING REQUIREMENT (PSBR)

Difference in the UK between the government's expenditure and revenue. It includes local authority expenditures.

PUBLIC UTILITIES

State or private sector enterprises providing services of public interest, e.g. electicity, gas, water, telecommunications.

PULSES

Edible beans, lentils and peas.

PUMP PRIMING

Government expenditure to stimulate a business recovery and achieve full employment.

PURCHASE FUND

Undertaking by a borrower to buy back a certain amount of an issue within a given period if the market price of the bonds falls below 100 per cent or below the issue price.

PUT OPTION

Option to sell stocks or commodities at an agreed price within a specified time, made in expectation of falling prices.

PWH

Per working hatch. Shipping term.

QUICK ASSETS

See LIQUID ASSETS.

QUINQUENNIAL REVISION

See TRIENNIAL REVISION.

QUOTA

(a) Quantitative limits on imports. May be applied to a specific product or a general group of products from a single country or a group of countries.

(b) Production target, or a limit on production.

(c) Country's subscription to the International Monetary Fund. 25 per cent used to be represented by gold (now by SDRs) and the remainder by a subscription in the country's domestic currency. The size of the country's quota governs its voting rights within the IMF.

QUOTATION

Current price or rate of a commodity, security or currency on the market place, or exchange, but not necessarily the price at which a trade will be made.

QUOTATION COMMITTEE

(a) In the UK the Stock Exchange committee responsible for reviewing and approving applications from a company to be quoted on the exchange.

(b) Committee responsible for official London Metal Exchange prices.

RALLY

Rise or recovery in prices or values after a decline.

RANs

Revenue anticipation notes issued by US states and municipalities.

RANGE

High and low prices, or high and low bids and offers recorded during a specified time.

RATING

Creditworthiness of a specific security issue or a particular borrower as evaluated by a ratings agency, e.g. in the US graded from 'triple A' downwards.

RAW MATERIALS

Unprocessed commodities. See PRIMARY COMMODITIES.

Ra

RAW VALUE
Value of unprocessed sugar. Basically the amount of raw sugar needed to make one pound (lb) of refined sugar.

REACTION
When prices decline after gaining or rise after falling.

REAL ESTATE INVESTMENT TRUST (REIT)
US property development and investment companies.

REAL GNP
True level of national output after subtracting inflation.

REAL INCOME/WAGES
Personal spending power or true wages received after adjusting for inflation.

REALISE
Sell an asset.

REALLOWANCE
In underwriting, a fixed percentage of the selling concession representing discounts between NASD members.

RECEIVABLES
Outstanding debts due to a corporation.

RECESSION
Decline in overall business activity, classically defined as two consecutive quarterly falls in real GNP.

RECOVERABLE RESERVES
Oil known to exist and be economically recoverable. Also known as proven reserves.

RECOVERY
See RALLY.

Re

RECOVERY FACTOR
Ratio of oil and/or gas reserves which can currently be recovered to estimated total deposits.

REDEMPTION
Exchange of one class of securities for another or for cash by the issuer, usually at maturity.

REDEMPTION PREMIUM
Excess of the price at which loans or securities may be redeemed by the borrower over the original, or the par value of the loan.

REDEMPTION YIELD
Current yield increased or diminished to take account of the capital gain or loss on redemption.

REDISCOUNT
Purchase before maturity by a central bank of a government obligation or other financial instrument already discounted in the money market.

RE-EXPORT
Export of imported goods or commodities without substantial processing or transformation.

REEF
Lode of gold-bearing quartz.

REEFER
Refrigerated cargo ship.

REFERENCE BANK(S)
Bank or group of banks whose interbank lending rates are used as a reference for determining the interest rate on a FLOATING RATE instrument.

Re

REFERENCE PRICE
Minimum import price for certain farm products under the EC Common Agricultural Policy. Normally based on an average of EC market or producer prices over a given period. Specifically it refers to a commodity of a prescribed quality which may be supported by intervention measures.

REFINERY
Equipment used to separate the various substances present in crude oil thus making them into usable products and feedstock.

REFLATION
The administered recovery of an economy. Also a type of inflation during a recovery period in which prices are restored to a desirable previous gradient by monetary policy.

REFUNDING
Rollover of (government) debt by replacing one issue by another, the maturity of which is deferred to a later date, typically by offering a straight exchange. Also the replacement of an issue by another bearing a lesser interest charge, thereby reducing the cost of servicing the debt. The latter is sometimes called refinancing.

REGISTERED COMMODITY REPRESENTATIVE
Person in the US who is registered with the Commodity Futures Trading Commission and the exchanges as seeking commodity business for his firm.

REGISTERED SECURITY
Security registered on the books of the issuing company in the name of the owner. Such ownership can only be transferred when endorsed by the owner.

Re

REGISTRATION

Requirement for a corporation to be listed in the US under the 1934 Securities Exchange Act before it can be admitted for dealings on a national security exchange. Public offerings of new securities by a corporation or outstanding securities by controlling shareholders must also be registered under the 1933 Securities Act. Similar rules with basically the same objectives exist in countries where there are exchanges and securities markets. However, the exact amount of information which must be disclosed and the different legal requirements can vary considerably between countries.

REGULAR WAREHOUSE

Warehouse or storage facility approved as the point from which actual futures delivery may take place.

REGULAR WAY DELIVERY

System in the US stock and bond markets whereby securities sold must be delivered by the selling broker to the purchasing broker and payment made by the fifth business day after the sale. Government bonds must be delivered the next business day after the transaction.

REGULARITY

In the US a processing plant, warehouse, mill, vault or bank that satisfies exchange requirements for financing, handling capacity and location, and which has been approved as acceptable for delivery of commodities against futures contracts.

REGULATED COMMODITIES

US futures markets in all commodities regulated since April 1975 under the Commodity Exchange Act as amended by the Commodity Futures Trading Act of 1974.

REGULATION (EC)

Acts of the EC Council of Ministers or the Commission which are totally binding and directly applicable in all member states.

Re

REGULATION M
Since April 1981, this gives the US Federal Reserve Board the power to regulate consumer leasing. Previously Regulation M covered the foreign activities of member banks. These are now covered by the International Banking Act of 1979 and the Monetary Control Act 1980.

REGULATION Q
US Federal Reserve power to impose interest rate ceilings on certificates of deposit and all time deposits. It is scheduled to be phased out by 1983.

REGULATION T
US Federal Reserve regulation limiting the amount of credit which can be advanced by brokers and dealers to customers to buy securities, or for margin requirements.

REGULATION U
US Federal Reserve regulation governing the quantity of credit a bank can provide to its clients seeking to buy securities.

REINSURER
Insurance concern operating in the reinsurance market whereby the initial insurer reinsures part of the original risk.

RELET
Term for a ship already on period commitment which is made available for a single voyage or period to a further charterer.

RENTE
(a) Undated French government bond.
(b) Annual income from an annuity or stocks; unearned income in general.

REPORTING LIMIT
Size of positions in a market at or above which daily details are required by commodity, delivery month and whether it is a hedging or speculative position.

REPURCHASE AGREEMENT

Usually involves US Treasury or federal agency securities. Generally transacted in denominations of five million dollars or more, these instruments are basically loan arrangements by which a holder sells the securities at a specified price under commitment to repurchase the same or similar securities at a later date. They are considered collateral for the transaction. Dealers in the New York money market use these arrangements to finance their positions. The Federal Reserve utilises such agreements to increase and withdraw bank reserves.

RESCHEDULING

Re-negotiation of terms and conditions of existing borrowings, with the objective of obtaining more favourable terms. See REFUNDING.

RESERVE CURRENCY

Currency which is internationally acceptable and is used by central banks to meet their financial commitments abroad.

RESERVE REQUIREMENT

Percentage of deposits that by law depository institutions (e.g. banks) must set aside in their vaults or with the central bank.

RESERVES (OFFICIAL)

Official foreign exchange reserves kept to ensure a government can meet current and near term claims. Official reserves are an asset in a country's balance of payments.

RESERVOIR ROCK

Porous and permeable rock, e.g. dolomite, sandstone or limestone, which contains hydrocarbons.

RESIDUAL FUEL OIL

Very heavy fuel oils produced from the residue after the fractional distillation process.

Re

RESISTANCE BARRIER
Price level above or below which a market may find difficulty in moving, partly the reflection of chartist sentiment.

RESTING ORDER
Order to purchase at a price lower than, or sell at a higher price than the prevailing market level.

RESTITUTIONS (EC)
EC export and other subsidies to Community processing industries.

RETAIL PRICE INDEX (RPI)
Measurement of the monthly change in the average level of prices at the retail level. It does not normally cover luxury goods.

RETAINED PROFITS
Profits earned for the equity holders in a company which are not distributed as dividend to shareholders. Accumulated retained profits are reserves on the balance sheet.

RETENDERING
In the US the right of holders of certain futures contracts who have been tendered a delivery notice via the clearing house to offer the notice for sale on the open market.

RETROCESSION
Decision by a reinsurer to reinsure part of the risk he has already accepted.

REVALUATION
Upward adjustment of a currency's parity or central rate.

REVERSE REPURCHASE AGREEMENT
Repurchase agreement initiated by a lender of funds. For the US Federal Reserve a means of temporarily draining reserves through the sale of securities which are later bought back. See REPURCHASE AGREEMENT.

REVERSIBLE LAY DAYS
If a shipper takes less time to load than agreed he may be allowed longer for unloading. See LAY DAYS.

REVOCABLE CREDIT
Credit given under a bill of exchange revocable at any time without notice.

REVOLVING CREDIT (REVOLVER)
Line of credit against which funds may be borrowed at any time, with regular scheduled repayments of a predetermined minimum amount.

RICE
Important cereal grain. Unprocessed but harvested rice is known as 'rough' or 'paddy' or 'padi'. Once the husk is removed it becomes 'brown' or 'cargo'. When the husk and outer bran layers have been removed it becomes 'milled' or 'polished' rice.

RIGHTS
Privileged stock or bond offering below market prices usually offered to existing shareholders or loan subscribers. A new offering on this basis is known as a rights issue.

RING
Designated area used for trading on the London Metals Exchange, the Zurich bourse and some other exchanges.

RISER (PIPE)
Wide diameter pipeline linking an offshore platform to a sub-sea wellhead or spur line.

RISK AVERSION
Degree to which an investor is unwilling to assume a risk.

RISK PREMIUM
Return or extra reward for assuming risks.

Ro

ROLLOVER

Extension of maturity debt by issuing fresh bonds, usually for exchange. See REFUNDING/RESCHEDULING.

RO/RO

Roll on/roll off ships, which allow containers to be driven on and off without the use of cranes.

ROUND LOT

Unit of trading on a stock exchange or any multiple of that unit, e.g. 100 stocks on the New York Stock Exchange.

ROUND TRIPPING

In the UK a situation where a company may decide to borrow from its bank using an existing line of short-term credit (overdraft) and then deposit those funds in the short-term money market for short-term gain. The situation arises when short-term money market rates are higher than those obtaining on an overdraft facility and a profit can be made from the interest rate differential.

ROUND TURN

Completed commodity futures transaction through an initial purchase and subsequent sale (or vice versa) of the same month, offsetting each other on the same market.

ROYALTY

Payment by a person or company to the owner of property or creator of original work for the privilege of using it commercially.

RPI

See RETAIL PRICE INDEX.

RUN

Process of widening, cumulative demands on a bank, or other financial institution, seeking the return of funds or money deposited with it.

Sa

RUNNING BALES
Term used in the cotton trade to designate the number of bales of cotton as they come from the gin in varying weights.

RUNNING YIELD
See CURRENT YIELD.

R/V
Round Voyage. A voyage from a certain area and back to the same area. Vessels can also be fixed for a number of round voyages and one and a half round voyages, etc.

RYE TERMS
Condition of the goods on arrival is guaranteed by the sellers. Shipping term.

SAFEGUARD
Temporary action to protect the domestic economy from a flood of imports.

SALVAGE
Reward for saving all or part of a ship or cargo from shipwreck.

SAMPLE GRADE
Usually the lowest quality of a commodity acceptable for delivery under a futures contract.

SAMURAI BOND
Bond issued in Japan by a foreign borrower, denominated in yen, which can be bought by non-residents of Japan. No withholding tax is payable.

SANTA FE TYPE VESSEL
See LIBERTY TYPE VESSEL.

Sa

SATURATION DIVING
Divers working and living under high pressure for long periods rather than undergoing decompression after every job.

SAVINGS AND LOAN ASSOCIATION
US national or state chartered institution holding savings deposits and primarily making funds available to the housing industry through home mortgages.

SAVINGS RATIO
Percentage of disposable personal income that is saved or used to repay debt.

SBM
Soya-bean meal. Shipping term.

SBT
Segregated ballast tanks. Shipping term.

SCALE DOWN
To buy at regular price intervals in a declining market. Scale up is to sell at similar regular price intervals in a rising market.

SCALPER
Speculator buying and selling rapidly with gains or losses.

SCHEDULED TERRITORIES
Remnant of the former Sterling Area group of countries. It comprises the UK including the Channel Islands and the Isle of Man, the Republic of Ireland, and Gibraltar.

SCHULDSCHEINDARLEHEN
Financial instrument in West Germany involving a loan against a borrower's note.

SCRIP
Subscription certificate. Used for a provisional document given to a person allotted shares. Also, more widely any form of security.

SCRIP ISSUE
Free share issue, sometimes made as a stock dividend.

SDR
See SPECIAL DRAWING RIGHT.

SEASONAL ADJUSTMENT
Statistical allowance for seasonal monthly or quarterly swings in the raw data of an economic series. Annual rate figures have no adjustment factor since the seasonal influence is no longer relevant.

SEASONED ISSUE
Outstanding securities issue, usually well received, which is already traded on the secondary market, when more of the same security is brought to market, especially in the US.

SEAT
Membership of a stock or commodity exchange or commodity market.

SECONDARY DISTRIBUTION
See SECONDARY OFFERING

SECONDARY MARKET
(a) Telephone/telex and over the counter market for the sale and purchase of international and foreign bonds or domestic securities after initial issue on primary markets. The proceeds of the sale are received by an investor and not by the corporation or governmental unit underlying the transaction.
(b) In commodities, sale or resale by an intermediary rather than a first-hand seller.

SECONDARY OFFERING
Also known as a secondary distribution. The redistribution in the US of a block of stock, normally of an established corporation, some time after it has been brought to market by a firm or group of securities firms. Normally a block too

large to be absorbed by the market in the regular course of trading.

SECONDARY RECOVERY
Technique for recovering oil or gas from a reservoir by artificially maintaining or enhancing the reservoir pressure through the injection of gas, water or other substances into the reservoir rock.

SECURED LOANS AND NOTES
Loans in support of which some specific property belonging to the debtor is charged.

SECURITIES & EXCHANGE COMMISSION (SEC)
Official US body established by the Securities Exchange Act of 1934. Charged with regulatory oversight and administering rules associated with all parts of the securities industry.

SEISMIC SURVEY
Survey to establish the structure of underground rocks by creating shock waves in the strata and then measuring the reflected signals, i.e. vibrations.

SELF-FINANCING
When a company finances investment programmes out of internally generated funds.

SELL DOWN
Portion of a new issue offered to likely participants outside the underwriting syndicate.

SELLERS' MARKET
Market in which sellers hold the advantage because buyers are prepared to buy, at existing prices, larger amounts than sellers are currently able to produce or prepared to market.

SELLERS' OPTION

Option for a seller to decide, provided the standard contract terms are observed, the time and place of delivery and/or the quality of commodity or security supplied in execution of an order.

SELLING GROUP MEMBERS

Those invited by a lead manager to place an issue. The group consists of all syndicate members plus other banks and securities dealers. Members report their subscription results to the lead manager and thereupon receive an allotment depending on their results and on their position and reputation as placers. They are allocated a set time, the selling period. Unlike syndicate members, they assume none of the risk of underwriting the securities.

SELLING HEDGE

Also known as a short hedge. Involves selling a futures contract as protection against a future fall in prices.

SENIOR ISSUE

Fixed income securities, the holders of which have priority over the claims of creditors.

SERIAL BONDS

Bonds with a series of staggered maturities, more frequently US municipal bonds than corporate.

SETTLEMENT DAY

See ACCOUNT DAY

SETTLEMENT PRICE

Average price at the close of a day's trading in commodities, usually used to set the next day's fluctuation limits and to determine margin calls on futures contracts.

SETTLEMENTS

Inter-central bank payments to cover external deficits and intervention debts.

Sh

SHARE CAPITAL
Total of shares authorised to be issued, or actually issued by a company. See PAID UP CAPITAL.

SHARE PREMIUM
Premium charged on the issue of shares in excess of their nominal value.

SHARE REGISTER
Register kept by a limited company giving details of shareholdings, including addresses of shareholders.

SHELTERDECK
Vessel which has a higher than normal superstructure above the main deck of the vessel. To be a true shelterdeck ship, a tonnage opening should be fitted and the end of the deck left unclosed. When cargo is carried in this space, the space is calculated in the ship's tonnage figures. If the space is open and unused, it is excluded from tonnage figures and no dues are charged on this space.

SHEX
Saturdays and holidays excluded. Shipping term.

SHINC
Saturdays, Sundays and holidays included. Shipping term.

SHIPBROKER
Agent for the shipowner or shipping company handling cargo space, insurance, freight, passengers, ship chartering.

SHORT ANCHOR
Very short term component of a US Treasury refunding package.

SHORT BILL
Bill of exchange payable on demand or within a very short time.

SHORT DATES
Standard Eurodeposit periods from overnight up to three weeks.

SHORT INTEREST
Number of stocks needed to be purchased to cover short sales.

SHORT POSITION
A situation where a commodity, currency or security has been sold and has to be cancelled out or covered by a corresponding purchase.

SHORT SALE
Sale of stocks, bonds, foreign exchange or commodities that the seller does not own, made in anticipation of a fall in prices.

SHORT TERM CAPITAL ACCOUNT
Balance of payments account depicting movements in short term funds.

SHORT TON
Ton of 2,000 lbs.

SIAC
Securities Industry Automation Corporation. An independent organisation established by the New York and American Stock Exchanges as a jointly owned subsidiary to provide automated data processing, clearing and communications services.

SIBOR
Singapore Interbank Offered Rate.

SID
Single decker. Shipping term.

SIGHT BILL
Bill of exchange payable immediately on demand.

SINKING FUND
Undertaking by a borrower, regardless of price movements in the secondary market, to redeem a certain amount of an

issue within a given period through payments to a special account.

SIPC
Securities Investor Protection Corporation. Established in US in 1970 to protect securities firms' customers from losses resulting from securities firms' financial failure. All US broker dealers are required to be members.

SITC
Standard International Trade Classification. A uniform system of presenting and reporting trade statistics.

SKIP DAY SETTLEMENT
On the US domestic market settlement which takes place one day later than the normal business date for settlement.

SLUICE GATE PRICE
Theoretical CIF import price on certain agricultural products used in calculating supplementary EC levies on imports of those products.

SLUMP
Severe or sustained stagnation in overall economic activity.

SMITHSONIAN AGREEMENT
Agreement of December 18, 1971 among the Group of Ten on major parity adjustments which included a devaluation of the US dollar against gold, a widening of parity bands to $2\frac{1}{4}$ per cent either side of par from 1 per cent, and the suspension of a 10 per cent US import surcharge.

SMITHSONIAN RATES
Exchange rates fixed by the Smithsonian Agreement by the Group of Ten signatories plus Switzerland, and subsequently by non-participating countries.

So

SNAKE
Co-ordinated float of a group of European currencies which can only move within prescribed limits against each other but which can float without prescribed limits against the US dollar and other non-member currencies. See EMS.

SOFT GOODS
Consumer or producer goods with a limited life, also called non-durable goods.

SOFT LOAN
Loan or credit granted at below market rates and often over a longer period than normal, especially to developing countries.

SOLAS
System under which tweendeck vessels can load bulk grains without fittings or bags while ensuring cargo stability. Shipping term.

SOUR CRUDE
High sulphur content crude oil.

SOUR GAS
Gas, either associated or natural, with a high sulphur content.

SOVEREIGN IMMUNITY
Legal doctrine which provides that in certain cases a sovereign state cannot be sued, or have its assets seized.

SOVEREIGN RISK
Risk of lending too much results in banks normally observing limits on the amount of lending they will make to any single government or organisation whose borrowing is guaranteed by that government. Such a sovereign risk is, however, more acceptable than one incurred on a loan not subject to a government guarantee.

Sp

SPARE CAPACITY
Margin of unused manufacturing capacity in an economy or company.

SPECIAL BID
Method of filling an order to buy a large block of stock on the floor of the New York Stock Exchange. The bidder pays a special commission to the broker representing him but the seller does not pay a commission. The special bid is made on the floor of the exchange at a fixed price which may not be below the last sale of the security or the current regular market, whichever is higher.

SPECIAL COMMITTEE ON AGRICULTURE (EC)
EC committee grouping the top agricultural experts in each of the national permanent delegations to the EC with national governmental and Commission representatives. Its task is to try to establish what is politically feasible in the EC agricultural sector.

SPECIAL DEPOSITS
Form of reserve requirement operated by a central bank, e.g. the Bank of England, under which banks may be required to maintain a percentage of their deposits at the central bank.

SPECIAL DRAWING RIGHT (SDR)
Intangible reserve asset created by the International Monetary Fund and allocated to the books of central banks in proportion to their quotas. Its value is a composite of the US dollar, West German mark, French franc, sterling and the yen.

SPECIFIC GRAVITY
Ratio of density of a substance at a particular temperature to the density of water at 4°C.

SPECULATOR
One who engages in speculation. A recognised participant in most markets.

SPIN OFF

Method used by a company to split its operations and assets by proportionately distributing to its own shareholders shares which it owns in another company. Sometimes called hive off.

SPLIT

Division of the outstanding shares of a corporation into a larger number of shares, although the proportional ownership of the shares is maintained.

SPLIT SPREAD

Normally applies to a Eurocredit with different spreads over LIBOR for different periods of the credit.

SPOT

(a) Price at which a currency or physical commodity is selling for immediate or very near delivery, i.e. two days in the case of foreign exchange. See CASH MARKET.

(b) Term for a ship available for charter in the immediate vicinity of a charterer's requirements for tonnage.

SPOUT TRIMMED (SPT)

A vessel loaded with a bulk cargo trimmed or levelled off. Commodities like grains are often spout trimmed which means they are loaded by a spout or chute which ensures level loading.

SPREAD

(a) Gap in a quotation between buying and selling prices e.g. the difference between the purchase of one futures delivery month against the sale of another delivery month of the same commodity.

(b) For new issues the flotation cost or the amount by which the offering price exceeds the proceeds received by the issuer.

SPUDDING IN

Starting to drill an oil/gas well by making a hole with a large diameter bit.

Sq

SQUARE
Occurs when purchases and sales are in balance, i.e. when a position is neither short nor long.

SQUEEZE
(a) Pressures exerted on one commodity's delivery, usually spot, when the price is exaggerated upwards against the rest of the market.
(b) Official action by a central bank or government to reduce supply in order to force up the price of money.

STABEX (EC)
EC programme for helping developing countries under the Lomé Convention. If export earnings fall below a certain level, financial assistance is available from the EC.

STAG
Operator who applies for a new security on the chance of selling it on allotment at a premium over the issue price.

STAGFLATION
Recession, stagnation or severe growth slowdown that is accompanied by steep inflation.

STANDARD & POOR'S
US securities ratings organisation for bonds etc. See also MOODY'S.

STANDBY CREDIT
Arrangement with a lender (either a group of banks, or the IMF in the case of a member country) that a fixed amount of credit will be available for drawing during a given period, if required.

STANPOOR'S
Composite index of 500 New York Stock Exchange common stocks published by Standard & Poor's.

STEM
> (a) In shipping, subject to availability of cargo.
> (b) In foreign exchange, the figure before the decimal point.

STEP OUT WELL
> A well drilled away from a discovery well to assess the reservoir area. Oil term.

STERILISATION PRESCRIPTIONS
> Short and medium term notes issued by the Swiss National Bank to soak up, and so control, money market liquidity.

STERLING AREA
> No longer in existence but was a group of Commonwealth and certain other countries which held a high percentage of their reserves in sterling, often on the basis of a Bank of England guarantee of value.

STL
> St Lawrence. Shipping term.

STOCK DIVIDEND
> Authorised but unissued shares paid to shareholders as a dividend. Similar to a split but involving a smaller increase in total shares outstanding.

STOCK EXCHANGE
> Organised trading floor for stock and share transactions.

STOCK OPTION
> Contract conferring the right to all or certain employees to buy or sell a specified number of shares at a certain price in a stipulated period.

STOCK-SALES RATIO
> Ratio of inventory (stocks) to turnover, measuring buoyancy in the business economy.

St

STOCK SPLIT

Division of the capital stock of a company into a greater number of shares without affecting the total capital amount.

STOCKY

Foreign exchange term for Swedish kroner.

STOP GO

Economic policy alternating periods of economic restriction and expansion.

STOP LIMIT

Stop order which becomes a limit order after the specified price has been reached.

STOP ORDER (STOP LOSS ORDER)

Order to a stock or commodity broker to buy or sell at the market when a given price threshold is reached.

STOPE

A place to extract ore inside a mine.

STOWED

Cargo packed and secured for a voyage.

STRADDLE

(a) In commodities, the simultaneous matching purchase of one delivery with the sale of another.

(b) In stock markets, a contract giving the holder the right to buy or sell at a certain price.

(c) In options trading, a simultaneously held 'put and call' giving the holder the right to buy and sell at a certain price.

STRAIGHT BOND

Bond, often a Eurobond, which is not convertible into equity. Some straights may be redeemed early through a purchase or sinking fund.

STRAIGHT RUN
Product made directly from crude oil by distillation but not cracked or reformed.

STRUCTURAL UNEMPLOYMENT
Unemployment resulting from a basic underlying change in the economy or a specific industry.

SUBJECT STEM
A vessel that has been chartered for business but without confirmation that the cargo will be available on time. Shipping term.

SUBORDINATED
Bonds with status junior to other current outstanding debt of the same issuer. In the event of bankruptcy, senior creditors are paid off first.

SUPER GOLD TRANCHE
Automatic drawing right with the IMF represented by reductions below 75 per cent of quota of the fund's holdings of a given currency. The member country can obtain funds if needed to the full amount represented by the super gold tranche without incurring any conditions.

SUPPLEMENTARY LEVY (EC)
Additional levy charged on imports of certain farm products under the EC's Common Agricultural Policy.

SUPPORT POINT
(a) Point at which a central bank may intervene in a currency, usually its own.
(b) Level at which market forces may combine to prevent further price declines for a currency or security.

SWAD
Salt water arrival draft. Shipping term.

Sw

SWAP
(a) Temporary purchase with guaranteed resale, or line of reserve currency credits between central banks. It can also cover the simultaneous exchange of securities.
(b) Foreign exchange price denoting the interest differential between two currencies for the same term.

SWEET CRUDE
Crude oil with a low sulphur content, such as those from North Africa, Nigeria and the North Sea.

SWITCHING
In commodities, the transfer of an open position into another delivery through the simultaneous liquidation of one futures commitment and the establishment of another in the same market.

SYNDICATE
Group of investment banks or financial institutions which guarantee to buy (underwrite) on a wholesale basis a new securities issue from the issuer and offer it for resale to investors. A group of banks which join together to raise medium term finance for governments, financial institutions or other entities via the Euromarkets.

SYNTHETIC FIBRES
See MANMADE FIBRES.

T/A
Transatlantic. Shipping term.

TAB
Tax anticipation bill, formerly a short term money instrument sold by the US Treasury to smooth the inflow of corporate tax payments. In the UK it is known as a tax reserve certificate.

TAFT-HARTLEY ACT

Primary law in US labour management relations endowing the executive branch of government with substantial powers to prevent and settle labour disputes, such as the imposition of cooling-off periods, usually 90 days, and the determination of collective bargaining procedures.

TAIL

Difference in US Treasury auctions between the average issuing price and the lowest accepted price (or stop out price).

TAKE DOWN

To receive and accept an allotment of shares or bonds in the primary market.

TAKE OUT

US term for cash surplus generated by the sale of one block of securities and the purchase of another at a lower price.

TANs

Tax anticipation notes issued in the US by states or municipalities in anticipation of future tax revenue.

TAP

To seek financing through the issue of shares, stock or bonds on stock markets or capital markets.

TAP STOCK

British government bond of short, medium or long term maturity, issued through the government broker at a stated price and used to control the market. Supplies to the market may be turned on or off, hence the term tap.

TARGET PRICE

(a) Overall common target wholesale price for grains under the EC Common Agricultural Policy. It is based on the desirable wholesale delivered price to Duisburg, which the EC views as the area of greatest cereal deficit.

T

(b) In the US the price basis used by government to assess payments to farmers to maintain parity with notional 1914 price levels.

TARIFF
Customs duty or border tax levied on imports.

TAX ANTICIPATION BILL
See TAB.

TCT
Timecharter trip. Shipping term.

TECHNICAL DECLINE (RALLY)
Movement in market prices reflecting the impact of technical internal market factors such as volume, short selling delivery conditions or chartist influence, as opposed to outside supply/demand factors.

TELEGRAPHIC TRANSFER (TT)
Transfer of funds from one bank to another by cable.

TEN (10) K
Detailed corporate annual reporting form required by the U S Securities and Exchange Commission. Basically similar but supplementary to the annual report.

TENDER
Notice of intent to deliver physical goods against a commodity futures contract. Also a means of offering bonds or treasury bills to the market, or inviting suppliers to offer plant or goods to meet requirements.

TENDER OFFER
In the US a public offer to buy shares for cash or other securities from existing shareholders of one corporation by another

company or organisation, under specified terms in force for a limited period.

TENDERABLE GRADES

Applies to commodities. Also called deliverable grades.

TENOR

Total time from issue to maturity of a financial instrument or security.

TERM BOND

Issue with all bonds maturing on the same date.

TERM FED FUNDS

US Federal funds sold for longer than the usual overnight.

TERM LOAN

Loan for a fixed period usually more than a year.

TERMINAL MARKET

Commodity market where physicals are exchanged for cash.

TERMS OF TRADE

Relationship between export and import price indices. If export prices rise more quickly, or fall at a slower pace than import prices, there is a favourable ratio.

TERRITORIAL WATERS

The United Nations Law of the Sea Convention adopted in April 1982 establishes a 12 nautical miles territorial sea zone, and a 200 nautical miles exclusive economic zone for coastal states. The convention has to be ratified by participating states.

TERTIARY RECOVERY

Oil or gas recovery from a reservoir in excess of that possible by primary and secondary recovery and requiring special techniques.

Te

TEU
Twenty foot equivalent units. The area of a container ship is given in TEUs. Shipping term.

THERMAL CRACKING
This occurs when basic hydrocarbon feedstock is broken down (cracked) to produce light products, through the sole use of heat and pressure, without employing a catalyst.

THI
Temperature Humidity Index in US weather reports indicating degree of discomfort for humans or livestock.

THIN MARKET
Market as a whole, or for a single commodity or security, in which there is little buying or selling interest, little volume or activity.

THIRD MARKET
In the US the trading of stock exchange listed securities in the over the counter market by non-exchange brokers and other investors.

THIRD WINDOW
Alternative low interest source of lending to developing nations by the World Bank.

THROUGH BILL OF LADING
Bill covering shipment on more than a single vessel, by different carriers or transport systems.

THROUGHPUT
Total amount of work and products processed by a plant, such as a car factory or an oil refinery, in a given period.

TICK
Price movement up or down.

TIED LOAN
Country to country loan requiring the recipient state to purchase goods or services from the donor.

TIGHT MARKET
Active and competitive market combining considerable volume with narrow spreads between bid and asked prices.

TIGHT MONEY
Monetary restraint policy restricting the availability of credit and usually forcing interest rates higher.

TIME DEPOSIT
Bank deposit of fixed maturity.

TIME (LIMIT) ORDER
Order to buy or sell on a market at a specific time. It may occur at a stated time of day, at the opening, close or mid-session or some time during a week. See LIMIT ORDER.

TIMECHARTER
Ship charter arranged for a fixed period. Payment is either in dollars per deadweight ton per month or dollars daily, but it excludes voyage costs. The charterer has the use of the vessel with the shipowner supplying the crew and provisions.

TIMES COVERED
Number of times the amount available for distribution, i.e. earnings, can be divided by the amount of the distribution, i.e. dividend.

TOMBSTONE
Advertisement for a stock, bond or syndicated credit issue, not including the issue price, appearing in newspapers and financial magazines as a matter of record. It usually describes the site and type of issue, and the composition of the syndicate.

To

TOM/NEXT
Simultaneous purchase of a currency for delivery the next business day and for the spot day or vice versa.

TONNE
See METRIC TON.

TOPPING UP
(a) After a ship has passed through the St Lawrence seaway it is topped up to full cargo capacity at ports at the mouth of the river.

(b) In finance, a clause whereby a borrower records his agreement to deposit further security if the lender asks for it.

TRADE BARRIER
Artificial restraint on the free exchange of goods and services between countries, usually in the form of tariffs, subsidies, quotas or exchange controls.

TRADE DATE
Day on which a deal is carried out or completed. The settlement date may be the same or later.

TRADE HOUSE
Trading concern acting on behalf of customers as well as on its own account.

TRADEABLE AMOUNT
Minimum quantity accepted for trading in a market.

TRADING LIMIT
(a) Maximum amount of a commodity which can be bought or sold by any individual in a single trading day.

(b) Maximum futures position permitted to be held by any individual.

(c) Maximum permitted price movements in any single day.

TRADING PAPER
Certificates of deposit expected to be traded by purchasers on Euromarkets.

TRADING POST
On the New York Stock Exchange the 23 trading positions, each trading some 75 stocks assigned to it.

TRAMCO VESSEL
Multi-purpose cargo ship of 7,000 to 10,000 dwt built in West Germany. Shipping term.

TRAMP VESSEL
Vessel engaged in casual trade, or upon charter party fixtures, each of which operates as a separate voyage and does not constitute part of a regular service. Shipping term.

TRANCHE
An agreed instalment of a credit or loan, which may be drawn down as required. Also refers to a country's drawings from the IMF which are made in tranches.

TREASURY BILL
Short term government bearer security (not more than one year, usually three to six months) sold on a regular basis and commanding a dominating position on money markets. It is sold at a discount from par being short term. The purchase and sale of such bills, i.e. through open market operation, form a key part of monetary policy.

TREASURY NOTE
One to 10 year US Treasury security.

TREASURY STOCK
In the US stock issued by a company but later reacquired. It can be held, retired or reissued. While held by the company it does not receive a dividend and cannot be used for voting purposes.

Tr

TRIENNIAL REVISION
Revision of IMF quotas is on a three (triennial) or five year (quinquennial) basis. Can be global or selective.

TRIGGER PRICE (EC)
Intervention price under the EC's CAP and commodity stabilisation funds. If prices fall below the set level, financial aid for the storage of the products concerned may be introduced or other measures taken.

TRIMMED
Levelling of a cargo after loading. Shipping term.

TRIPCHARTER
Charter arranged for a voyage specifying delivery and redelivery ports or areas. Payments in dollars per deadweight ton or dollars daily exclude voyage costs.

TRIPLE NINE
Highest degree of gold purity or 99.9 per cent pure gold.

TSP
Triple Super Phosphate fertiliser. Shipping term.

TURNKEY
An industrial plant which is completely operational when it is handed over to the buyer.

TWEENDECKER
Ship having one or more decks below the main deck.

TWO-TIER MARKET
Dual exchange rate system under which one tier is openly responsive to market pressure and the other is insulated by government intervention or control. e.g., Belgian financial and convertible francs.

TWO WAY MARKET
Market where dealers quote both buying and selling rates.

ULCC
Ultra large crude carrier. Generally means a crude oil tanker of 350,000 deadweight tons or above. See also VLCC.

ULLAGE
Distance between top of cargo and the hatches. Shipping term.

UNCTAD
United Nations Conference on Trade and Development. Established in 1964 to promote better international trading conditions for developing countries and to help raise their standard of living.

UNDATEDS
See IRREDEEMABLES.

UNDERSUBSCRIBED
See OVERSUBSCRIBED.

UNDERVALUED
See OVERVALUED.

UNDERWRITER
One who undertakes to place a certain amount of a share, stock or bond offering, by purchasing them for resale to investors. The offering may be purchased outright or through a syndicate.

UNEMPLOYMENT RATE
Ratio of jobless workers to the registered civilian labour force, usually seasonally adjusted.

UNFUNDED DEBT
See FLOATING DEBT.

UNIFIED BUDGET
US budgetary format covering receipts and outlays for federal and trust funds after deducting the transactions that flow between them.

Un

UNIT OF ACCOUNT
(a) A Monetary Unit widely used in the EC until 1979 and valued at one pre-Smithsonian dollar. It was then superseded for most transactions, including agriculture, by the European Currency Unit.

(b) A composite unit used to denominate some Eurobond issues or any hypothetical composite unit of currency measurement, e.g. SDRs.

UNIT OF TRADING
Minimum quantity in which trading can take place in a commodity or security.

UNIT TRUST
British equivalent of a mutual fund.

UNITARY WAGE RATE
Average hourly wage rate paid to a blue-collar worker in US manufacturing industry.

UNLOAD
Market term for dumping a substantial amount of a commodity, currency, security or other goods on a market at a low price with intent to

(a) Simply dispose of the asset being sold at any cost.

(b) Make a profit by low price volume sales, thus undercutting other market suppliers.

UNSECURED LOANS AND NOTES
Securities issued by a company without specifically charging all or any of its assets.

UNWINDING
Disengagement of a financial or a leads-and-lags speculative position.

US AT
US Atlantic ports. Shipping term.

US G
> US Gulf ports. Shipping term.

USNH
> US north of Hatteras. Hatteras is a port above the US Gulf and USNH covers such ports as New York, Boston, Philadelphia, Baltimore, Norfolk, Newport News and Portland, Maine. Also referred to as US Northern Range. Shipping term.

USNP
> US North Pacific ports. Shipping term.

USSH
> US ports south of Hatteras. Shipping term.

USURY
> Charging of excessive or unreasonable rates of interest.

VALUE ADDED TAX
> See VAT

VALUE DATE
> In the Eurocurrency and foreign exchange markets refers to the delivery date of funds to settle the transaction. In the Eurobond market the value date falls seven calendar days after the deal is struck, regardless of holidays.

VALUE SPOT
> Spot deal for settlement in two trading days.

VARIABLE (IMPORT) LEVY
> Customs duty rate which varies in response to some internal price criterion.

VARIABLE MARGIN CALL
> Call made in a clearing house to a clearing member during trading, when price movements have substantially reduced

V

Va

the clearing member's margin deposits. It is payable within the hour.

VARIABLE RATE
(a) Financial instrument or security bearing a variable interest rate. Can be applied to Certificates of Deposit issued for a normal minimum period of 360 days with the interest rate set at a specified spread over the current rate of 90-day CDs. Such CDs are adjusted every 90 days.
(b) In the UK may be applied to the innovative bonds introduced by the Government in 1977 whereby the rate of interest on the stock varies in line with the three months Treasury Bill rate. Interest is payable at half per cent above the bill rate.

VARIABLE RATE MORTGAGE
Domestic housing mortgage with an interest rate which fluctuates during the life of the mortgage, normally in line with a chosen market rate or index.

VAT
Value Added Tax. System of taxing products on the amount of value added at each stage of their production and exchange.

VELOCITY OF MONEY
Rate at which a unit of money is used within a given time. It is usually measured as the ratio of gross national product to the money stock. An increase in the velocity of money can reduce the effectiveness of a restrictive monetary policy.

VENTURE CAPITAL
Also called risk capital. Funds used for investment in companies where there is a degree of financial risk in the initial stages, e.g. companies exploiting new technological processes.

VISCOSITY
Measures the resistance of a fluid to motion or flow; as the temperature rises the viscosity normally decreases.

Vo

VISIBLE BALANCE (OF TRADE)
Country's trade in exports and imports of merchandise goods.

VISIBLE SUPPLY
(a) Known supply of commodities at the main production and storage centres.
(b) In the US new municipal bond issues coming to the market within 30 days.

VLCC
Very large crude carrier. Tanker capable of carrying large amounts of crude oil. Usually a minimum of 175,000 dwt would be necessary to qualify a vessel as a VLCC. See also ULCC.

VOLATILE MARKET
Sensitive market changing direction rapidly and erratically.

VOLATILITY
Ease with which a product begins to vaporise. Volatile substances have high vapour pressures, and therefore boil at relatively low temperatures.

VOLUNTARY LIQUIDATION
See BANKRUPTCY.

VOSTRO ACCOUNT
Account maintained abroad by a bank in the currency of the country in which the account is held. The bank holding the account would refer to it as a vostro account while the bank depositing the funds would refer to it as a nostro account. See NOSTRO ACCOUNT.

VOYAGE CHARTER
Ship charter arranged to carry a cargo on a single voyage between specified ports or areas. Payment, usually on either a cargo ton basis or on a cubic capacity basis, includes voyage costs.

Vo

VOYAGE COSTS
Vessel costs comprising bunkers, port and canal charges.

VOYAGE POLICY
Marine insurance policy issued for one particular voyage only.

WAGE DRIFT
Difference between basic wages and actual earnings, usually reflecting overtime, bonus payments, etc.

WAIVER CLAUSE
In marine insurance a provision enabling either party to take steps to reduce the impact of a loss without prejudice.

WAREHOUSE RECEIPT
Document providing proof of ownership of a specified quality and quantity of a commodity at a designated warehouse, e.g. LME warrant for metals.

WARRANT
Certificate conferring on the holder limited or perpetual rights to buy common stock or other securities, or to subscribe to a new issue.

WATER INJECTION
Process of pumping water into the reservoir rock to maintain pressure.

WAX
Solid hydrocarbon found in certain crude oils. Wax deposits in pipelines and equipment can cause exploitation and refining problems.

WCSA
West Coast South America. Shipping term.

WEATHER WINDOW

Time in the month or year when weather conditions are suitable, or likely to be so, for various offshore operations, e.g. platform installation.

WEEKLY RETURN

Series of statistics issued weekly e.g. summarising balance sheet position of most central banks.

WELL LOGGING

Comprehensive record of data obtained when drilling a well, providing a very detailed image of the underground rock formation.

WELLHEAD

Control equipment fitted to the top of a well casing, incorporating outlets, valves, blowout preventer, etc.

WET NATURAL GAS

Natural gas with large amounts of associated liquids. A wet gas may suggest the gas is being recovered from the vicinity of an oil reservoir.

WHEAT

Major export grain in world trade. Main US export categories consist of Hard Red, Winter Wheat, Hard Red Spring, Durum, White and Soft Red Winter. Winter wheat is planted in the autumn and harvested in the late spring and summer of the following year. Spring wheat is planted in the spring and harvested the same year.

WHEN ISSUED

Short for 'when, as and if issued'. Hypothetical price of a share not yet issued, often in a stock split. Conditional deals in the stock may take place on this basis.

W

Wh

WHOLESALE PRICE INDEX
See WPI.

WILDCAT
Exploration well drilled without knowledge of what the underlying rock formation may contain.

WILD WELL
Well which is out of control and blowing fluid or gas from the down hole reservoir.

WILDCAT APPRAISAL WELL
Well drilled with a minimum of preliminary information about the underground formation. Normally used after a wildcat well has shown signs of oil or gas.

WINDFALL (PROFIT)
Unexpected profit.

WINDOW DRESSING
Steps by banks and companies to present their accounts in a favourable light, often by raising additional short term funds.

WINZE
In mining, excavation of a reef made downwards to connect drives on different levels.

WIRE HOUSE
In the US, a member of an exchange with an internal communications network.

WITHHOLDING TAX
Tax on interest or dividend payments remitted to persons residing outside the country levying the tax; also tax deduction at source.

WORKING BALANCE

Discretionary currency component of a central bank's overall monetary reserves.

WORKING CAPITAL

Surplus of current assets over current liabilities, which provides the net resources with which a company can finance day to day operations.

WORKING CONTROL

Number of shares needed to control the activities of a corporation. In theory this is 51 per cent of all voting shares. In practice it can be less, sometimes considerably less, due to the distribution of stock ownership.

WORLD BANK

Main international agency for channelling aid funds for capital and human resource projects to developing countries. Set up under the BRETTON WOODS agreement of 1944 which also established the International Monetary Fund. The bank may channel private funds and make loans from its own resources. It also raises money by selling bonds on the world market. The official title is International Bank for Reconstruction and Development.

WORLD FOOD PROGRAMME

Multilateral food aid organisation set up by the Food and Agriculture Organisation and the United Nations in 1962 to help less developed countries and deal with food emergencies.

WORLDSCALE

Freight index designed to express tanker rates, irrespective of vessel size and route, in terms of the costing of a standard vessel. It is customary to negotiate levels of freight for tankers in terms of a percentage of the worldscale freight rates which are given in dollars. Thus worldscale 100 means the rate is as published by the Association of Ship Brokers and Agents

Wp

(Worldscale) Incorporated in New York, and by the International Tanker Nominal Freight Scale Association in London; Worldscale 200 would mean double the published rate. Worldscale replaced the earlier Intascale (International Tanker Nominal Rate Scale) and ATRS (American Tanker Rate Schedule) in 1969.

WPI

Wholesale Price Index. Typically anticipates movements in in the consumer price index by two to three months. Usually divided into foods and industrial products.

WRITE DOWN

To reduce the value of an asset by taking account of depreciation, or some other significant erosion of the asset's value.

WRITE OFF

Book-keeping action which, at one stroke, depreciates an asset out of the balance sheet.

WWD

Weather working days. This usually qualifies Shex or Shinc and means the exclusion of time lost through bad weather. Shipping term.

YANKEE BOND

Bond issued in the US by a foreign borrower in US currency and registered with the Securities and Exchange Commission. No withholding tax is payable.

YARD

Foreign exchange market term for one milliard (billion).

Ze

YEARLING

Stock issued by British municipal authorities for a period of one year and quoted either on the stock exchange or in the discount market.

YIELD

Percentage return on an investment, usually an annual rate.

YIELD TO MATURITY

Takes into account for a bond the price discount or the premium over the face value. It is larger than the current yield when the bond sells at a discount and smaller than the current yield when the bond sells at a premium.

Z CERTIFICATES

Certificates issued by the Bank of England in lieu of stock certificates to discount houses to facilitate their dealings in short dated stock. The certificates are issued as soon as a transfer of stock is lodged with the bank and can be split into smaller denominations if required. They are readily acceptable as collateral against loans.

ZERO COUPON

Discount basis corporate credit instrument issued with imputed interest calculated on the price paid by the buyer and the par value at which the bond will be redeemed. Typically such a bond would be issued in the amount of 200 million U S dollars, the price paid at redemption. It would provide the borrower with an immediate cash amount of less than half the value.

X
Y
Z